For Bird Lovers of All Ages

Wild About Michigan Birds

by Adele Porter

Adventure Publications
Cambridge, Minnesota

This book is dedicated to Byron, Elizabeth and Rachael. Wamlati!

The passion and dedication of a single individual can impact generations. Bertha Daubendiek, (1936–2005), of Avoca, Michigan was an inspiration as vibrant and rare as the native lands she loved. Bertha not only recognized the importance of living land museums, she took action to ensure that, wherever she could, they remained for tomorrow's children. It is to Bertha Daubendiek and the children of Michigan that I also dedicate this book: to a woman that cared deeply about the natural world and its future and to the children to which that future belongs.

Acknowledgments

My sincere thanks to the countless professionals and volunteers that have contributed their time, energy, and field data to state and federal reports, bird atlases and other citizen science projects. The collaborative efforts of wildlife professionals and volunteers across North America, as well as globally important migratory wintering areas, provide vital information to the life histories and population status of birds. These resources have been imperative to the writing of *Wild About Michigan Birds*.

Carrol Henderson, Minnesota DNR Nongame Wildlife Program:
Thank you for your continued support and allowing the use of your photographs of the Handsaker egg collection.

Friends, the neighborhood gang, and the teachers and students that shared their ideas and support:
Thank you for your invaluable enthusiasm and input.

Edited by Gretchen Jensen, Anthony Hertzel and Brett Ortler

Cover design by Lora Westberg

Book design, nest, migration map and habitat map illustrations by Jonathan Norberg

Habitat Café, feather, exterior and interior of bird illustrations by Julie Martinez; range maps and bird silhouette illustrations by Anthony Hertzel; cartoon bird illustrations by Brenna Slabaugh; child's nest drawing by Emily Connick

Photo credits by photographer and page number:
Egg photos: Chester A. Reed, *North American Birds Eggs:* 47 **R. L. Ridgway,** *Life Histories of North American Birds:* 53, 59, 61 **all other egg photos from the Handsaker Egg Collection taken by Carrol Henderson**
Rick and Nora Bowers: 134 (main) **Dudley Edmondson:** 44 (female), 60 (both), 136 (soaring) **Gijsbert van Frankenhuyzen/DPA*:** 102 (in flight) **John Gerlach/DPA*:** 40 (main) **Carrol Henderson:** 152 (winter), 164 (in flight), 178 (gosling) **Adele Porter:** 113 (Canada anemone) **Johann Schumacher/CLO*:** 158 (female) **Brian E. Small:** 70 (female), 128 (main), 168 (winter) **Alan Stankevitz:** 32 (both), 48 (both), 50 (fanned tail), 58 (main), 68, 76 (female), 80 (main), 92, (juvenile), 96, 98 (both), 100 (main), 106 (spitting pellet), 116 (main), 118, 122 (horns), 128 (in flight), 130 (main), 132 (both), 140 (both), 150, 172 (in flight), 180 (feeding), 184 (in flight), 186 (in flight) **Stan Tekiela:** 6 (Trumpeter Swans, Eastern Bluebird), 7 (Mallard, Indigo Bunting), 13 (American Kestrel), 14 (American Bittern), 27 (tamarack trees), 30 (both), 36 (main), 38 (both), 40 (female), 42 (both), 44 (main), 46 (both), 50 (main, crest), 52, 54 (all), 56, 58 (in flight), 64 (hawk nest), 70 (main), 72, 76 (main), 78 (both), 80 (female), 82 (both), 84 (both), 86 (both), 88 (both), 90 (main), 92 (main), 94 (side profile), 102 (all), 104 (main), 106 (main), 108 (all), 110, 113 (American Goldfinch in winter), 116 (male winter, female), 120 (both), 124 (both), 126, 130 (injury-feigning display), 136 (main, bottom inset), 138 (both), 144 (Bald Eagle), 148 (both), 152 (main), 154 (all), 156 (both), 160 (both), 162 (both), 164 (main, female), 166 (both), 168 (main), 170 (both), 172 (main), 174 (main), 176, 178 (main, in flight), 180 (main, fishing), 182 (both), 184 (main, aigrettes), 186 (main) **Brian K. Wheeler:** 100 (soaring), 134 (female) **Jim Zipp:** 7 (hawk's tail), 34 (both), 36 (inset), 74 (both), 94 (main), 100 (juvenile), 104 (landing), 122 (main), 134 (wheeling), 158 (main)
*DPA: Dembinsky Photo Associates; CLO: Cornell Laboratory of Ornithology

10 9 8 7 6 5

Wild About Michigan Birds
First Edition 2009, Second Edition 2014
Copyright © 2009 and 2014 by Adele Porter
Published by Adventure Publications, an imprint of AdventureKEEN
310 Garfield Street South
Cambridge, Minnesota 55008
(800) 678-7006
www.adventurepublications.net
Printed in China
ISBN 978-1-59193-450-9 (pbk.); ISBN: 978-1-59193-617-6 (ebook)

Thundering birds. Booming birds. Drumming birds.
Stompin', whistlin' and jazzin' birds.

MICHIGAN BIRDS

How to Use Your Book

Wild About Michigan Birds makes it easy to learn fascinating facts about 70 species of birds. You'll find identification tips and information on each species' favorite foods, interesting behaviors, songs and calls, life cycle, migration patterns and more.

The book is organized by habitat—the type of natural environment the bird calls home. It is divided into four sections, one for each of Michigan's four major habitats:

- Coniferous Forests
- Deciduous Forests
- Prairies
- Water Areas

Within each habitat section, you'll find the birds that live there arranged by size—smallest to largest—according to their length and wingspan.

For a list of the species in this book and the pages on which they appear, turn to the Table of Contents (pages 4–5). The Index (page 199) provides a handy reference guide to the species in alphabetical order. A taxonomic listing (scientific classification) of the birds is on page 198.

About Birds The beginning of this book shows the amazing characteristics that make birds unique. It explains how each part of a bird is designed to help it survive. You will also find clues to what is wild, what is a nongame bird and what is a game bird species.

How to Watch Birds Starting on page 14, this section gives you detective skills to find birds while being respectful to wildlife and the home we both share—Michigan!

When to Watch Birds When are the best times and seasons to spy on different birds? This section, starting on page 16, helps you understand why some birds can be seen at certain times of the day or year.

Where to Watch Birds Turn to page 20 to learn about our state's major land regions, and tips on where to find birds in each one.

Note From the Publisher *We received so much feedback regarding how our first edition of* Wild About Michigan Birds *was being used by both children and adults, that we decided to include "all ages" when addressing our audience. We are still leaving the "kid appeal" in the book as we think it's very important that bird watching is developed and shared by young and old. Hopefully, all users will appreciate the birds even more after referencing this information-packed resource.*

Table of Contents

*Mixed forest species

Watch for these friends!

Birding Tip

Great ideas for bird watching fun.

Did You Know?

Gee-whiz facts that'll WOW the whole family.

Do the Math

Brain-teasing bird math.
(Don't tell, but the answers are on pages 194-195.)

Gross Factor

Disgusting but interesting facts guaranteed to make your parents gag.

History Hangout

Cool details from the past such as where a bird's name comes from.

Unsolved Mystery

Puzzles and oddities that have left scientists baffled—maybe you'll discover the solutions.

About Birds

Chickadees, Swans and Hawks. What Makes Us Birds?

Black-capped Chickadee

Trumpeter Swans

Cooper's Hawk

Feathers Birds are the only living creatures that grow feathers. They have six basic kinds. Each one helps the bird with a special job: flight, warmth, protection, balance or flotation. The color and pattern of a bird's feathers can also help you identify which species you are watching. Learn more about feathers on page 10.

Great Gray Owl

Ears Yes, birds have ears under their cheek feathers. Some owls and hawks have amazing ears. Feathers arranged in a disk around the bird's face funnel sound to its ears, helping it hear better.

Lungs with air sacs Birds are equipped with two lungs with special balloon-like air sacs that can spread out into other parts of their bodies. This extra capacity allows a bird to store more air, push air through the lungs better and send more oxygen to its cells. This is important during long migration flights.

Eastern Bluebird

Bones Most birds have strong, flexible skeletons of hollow or semi-hollow bones with many air spaces. This helps them weigh less and—you guessed it—means lighter baggage for flying. For birds that spend a lot of time in the air, this is very important.

Oil Gland To keep its feathers in good condition, a bird spreads oil on its feathers. It gets the oil from the uropygium gland above its rump. The bird rubs oil on its beak, then spreads the oil over its feathers. Cleaning and arranging feathers in this way is called "preening."

Feet Most birds have four toes. Not all, though. Killdeer have just three toes, and all three face forward so the Killdeer can run fast! Toe arrangement can vary. A bird can have three toes in front and one in the back, or two toes in front and two in the back. This arrangement can tell you where the bird lives and how it gets around. You can get more clues about how and where the bird lives by looking at its feet. Are the feet webbed? Do they have large talons (claws)? Some birds have special toes that help them walk upside down, or hang onto a tree while pecking out a hole.

Red-tailed Hawk

Hawk's tail

Downy Woodpecker

Tail How does a bird steer or put on the brakes while flying? By spreading out its tail and adjusting its wing feathers! Each bird species has a tail designed to help it survive. A woodpecker's tail is stiff and pointed. This helps it brace itself against tree trunks while looking for food.

Songs and Calls Birds do not have vocal chords. They have a special voice box called a syrinx. They inflate air sacs to put pressure on the muscles of the syrinx, which makes a range of different sounds. Nearly all birds have some sort of call, but not all birds sing. Calls are short and used to signal danger, warn other birds to stay away or announce mealtime. They often sound the same from one species to another. Different bird species can use and understand the same calls. *Songs* are sung mostly by males and used to attract a mate or defend their territory. These songs are complex and are only understood by birds of the same species. Try doing what birds do: sing more than one note at a time, each note at a different intensity and compose 1,000 different phrases! Wow!

Mallard

Bald Eagle

Wings Flying, diving, swooping, hovering, escaping a predator, even landing...a bird depends on its wings, which are powered by large, strong muscles anchored to the breast bone. The shape of a bird's wings can tell you a lot about where it lives, what it eats and how it catches its prey. For example, pointed wings indicate a fast flier. Large, broad wings are common among big soaring birds, while birds that maneuver around trees in a forest have short, broad wings.

Crop and Gizzard How does a bird chew food without teeth? For some birds, the food first goes into a sack called a crop, which is located near the esophagus. From there, it is sent into a two-part stomach, where the gizzard grinds it up into smaller pieces. Some birds eat gravel or eggshells (substitute teeth) that stay in their gizzards for grinding hard-to-digest food.

Beak The shape and length of a bird's beak are clues to what and how it eats. How different can beaks be? Spoon, fork, knife, straw, strainer, fish net, tweezers, pliers, nutcracker, saw and chopsticks are a few different styles. Hungry? Select your dinnerware!

American White Pelican

Anatomy

It's easier to identify birds and talk about their characteristics if you know the names of their different parts. The following illustrations will help you understand basic bird anatomy. Because these images are composites of many species, they shouldn't be confused with any actual bird.

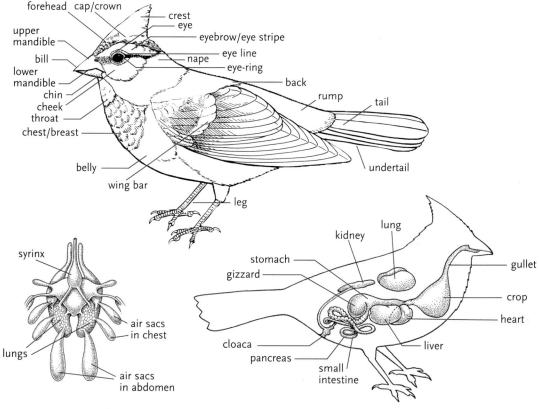

Eggs

Unlike Michigan mammal mothers, which give birth to squirming, squalling babies, female birds lay eggs. The shell is made of calcium (the same thing bones are made of) and protects the young bird developing inside it. The shape of the egg makes for a strong shell. It is sturdy enough for parent birds to sit on and incubate (keep warm), yet fragile enough for baby birds to break through at hatching. Some birds lay colorful eggs. The colors can hide the egg from predators or help parents identify imposters.

Almost all parent birds develop a "brood patch" on their chest or belly when incubating their eggs. The feathers either fall off or are plucked out. Blood vessels next to this bare spot help keep the eggs warm. Inside the egg, the yolk is the baby bird's main source of food. The egg white provides water and protein. This food, together with a temporary egg tooth, helps the chick free itself from the shell.

Robin eggs

Nests

Bird nests are amazing. Imagine building your house strong enough to survive a storm, large enough for your growing family, insulated—and waterproof. Now, imagine finding all the materials from the natural habitat where you live. Birds do!

Just as there are different kinds of birds, there are different types of nests. Some bird species, including the Killdeer and Horned Lark, prefer a simple **ground nest** scraped out of the earth. Birds with such nests may have eggs shaped to spin rather than roll away.

To build a nest that floats on water or balances on a cliff or bridge takes some fancy work. A **platform nest** may be built of small twigs and branches that form a simple base, with a dip in the middle to nestle the eggs.

Cup nests are used by most songbirds. They have a solid base attached to a tree, shrub or ledge. Sturdy sides are made by weaving grasses, twigs, bark or leaves tightly together. A soft, inner lining of feathers, fur or plant material keeps the eggs and young birds cozy.

Keeping a nest safe from predators calls for hanging out at the edge. A **pendulous nest** looks like a sock hanging at the end of a tree branch. It takes nearly a week for Baltimore Orioles to weave together the fibers of their strong watertight nests. They are such good tailors, it even feels like a soft sock!

Cavity nests are used by Pileated Woodpeckers, Eastern Bluebirds and many other woodland birds. Usually chipped into a tree trunk or branch, cavity nests often have a small entrance hole that leads to an inner room. A Belted Kingfisher builds its cavity nest into a cliff or riverbank, with a long tunnel leading to the nursery.

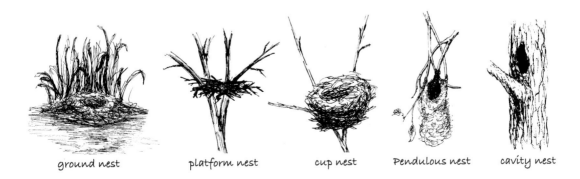
ground nest   platform nest   cup nest   Pendulous nest   cavity nest

Feathers

When dinosaurs roamed the Earth there also lived a prehistoric, crow-sized animal with feathers; scientists believe it was related to reptiles, and have named it **Archaeopteryx** (ar kay op tehr icks) from its fossil remains. Archaeopteryx was one of the first known bird species.

Today, birds still have characteristics of their distant relatives. Reptiles have scales of solid keratin. Bird feathers are also formed of keratin, but in strands, which are much lighter. Birds are the only animals on Earth with feathers!

Mallard

Feathers help a bird fly, stay warm and dry, and protect their skin. Feathers allow birds to swim through the water and fly through the air with less friction (which makes these jobs much easier). For some birds, such as owls, feathers quiet the sound of their flight. Feathers can be camouflaged, to help a bird hide from predators, or occur in bright colors to show off during courtship. Whew—feathers do a lot for birds!

What do birds do when their feathers start to get old? They molt (or shed) the old ones and replace them with new feathers one or two times each year. To keep their balance in flight, the feathers are shed a few at a time, in the same place on each side of the body.

Have you noticed the "goose bumps" on the skin of a chicken from the grocery store? The bumps, called papillae, are where feathers grow out of the skin. At the bottom of each of the papillae are ligaments (similar to muscles) that the bird uses to move each feather on its own, an important function when it needs to turn in flight or slow down!

Northern Cardinal

Did You Know? In herons, the middle foot claw has a comb-like serrated (jagged) edge used as a preening tool. This is called a pectate claw or feather comb. Herons use this claw to keep their feathers in top condition.

CONTOUR Feathers: Zipped in Place

Contour feathers overlap each other to give birds a streamlined body shape (a contour) for less friction, faster flight, and faster diving in the water. Contour feathers are found on the body, wings and tail. Contour feathers have a central shaft (rachis) with vanes on each side. Attached to the vanes are barbs. On each side of the barbs are small barbules that make a "zipper" to hold the feather barbs together. When the barbs unzip, the bird uses its beak to zip them back together while preening.

DOWN FEATHERS: Keeping Warm

Down feathers do not "zip" together like contour feathers, but stay fluffy. The air spaces hold the bird's body heat close like a warm blanket. Young birds often have down first, to keep their small bodies warm until their contour and other body feathers grow in. Adult birds' down feathers are located under their contour feathers.

SEMIPLUME FEATHERS: Support & Warmth

Semiplume feathers, which are found beneath the contour feathers, are a cross between a contour and a down feather. They have a stiff shaft, but also have soft down vanes that act like extra insulation.

FILOPLUME FEATHERS: Information Receivers

Filoplume feathers are tiny, hair-like feathers comprised of a long central shaft tipped with a tuft of barbules. They help a bird adjust the position of its flight feathers. These sensitive feathers move with the slightest breeze, sending information to the nerve cells at their bases. Vibrations from the filoplume feathers tell the bird when to adjust its contour feathers for better flight.

BRISTLE FEATHERS: Sense, Guard and Guide

Bristle feathers are stiff, hair-like feathers with a firm central shaft. They are found near the eyes, nostrils and beak, and may help protect the bird's eyes, help it to locate food, and funnel prey (such as flying insects) into its mouth.

POWDER DOWN FEATHERS: Talcum Powder Protection

Powder down feathers, found on birds such as Great Blue Herons (pg. 186) and Great Egrets (pg. 184), are never shed, but grow all the time. The ends break down into a waxy powder that protects the bird's skin from moisture and damage.

What is Wild?

Is your pet parakeet wild? It may act wild at times, but pets and farm animals are not wild. They are domesticated animals that depend on people for survival. Wild birds find their own food, water, shelter and a place to nest and raise their young.

Wild birds are not owned by people. They are a part of the greater global environment. In Michigan, wildlife biologists and managers study wild birds and their habitats. The information is used to make laws that protect wildlife and wild places. Conservation officers make sure everyone follows these rules, and you can help! Law-breakers can be turned in to the Michigan Department of Natural Resources (DNR) by calling the Report All Poachers tip line, 1-800-292-7800. People that call remain unidentified. Together, we can make sure Michigan birds are around for a long time.

Leave Wild Things Wild

Wild birds and animals were once considered unlimited resources. They were killed for their meat, feathers and hides without seasons or limits. By the late 1800s, unregulated market hunting (along with habitat destruction) caused many species—from the American Bison to the Great Egret—to almost disappear forever. The Passenger Pigeon, which once darkened the skies with its huge flocks, eventually became extinct.

Fortunately, laws like the Lacey Act and the Migratory Bird Treaty Act helped protect other wild birds before it was too late. These laws governed the harvest of migratory birds, including their eggs, nests and feathers. Today, many state and federal laws protect wild birds, animals and the habitats they need to survive.

Great Egret

The eggs shown in this book are from a famous collection of eggs gathered by Iowa farmer Ralph Handsaker in the late 1800s and early 1900s. Although wild bird eggs are now protected, in that era collecting eggs was a popular hobby for naturalists. Handsaker's collection consists of nearly 4,000 eggs from 400 species of birds found around the world. It is the focal point of the book *Oology and Ralph's Talking Eggs* by biologist Carrol Henderson. The collection is now at the Peabody Museum of Natural History at Yale University.

It's tempting to enjoy nature by taking it home with us. But it's important to keep wild things wild. Leave eggs, nests and baby birds in their natural habitat.

Game or Nongame Wildlife?

Ring-necked Pheasant

Wildlife that can be hunted under Michigan law, such as the Ring-necked Pheasant, is called **game wildlife**. The Michigan Department of Natural Resources (DNR) regulates hunting so it does not threaten game bird populations. For their part, hunters buy licenses and stamps, and pay special taxes on hunting gear; this raises millions of dollars for habitat protection and management that benefits all wildlife.

Birds that cannot be hunted legally are considered **nongame wildlife**. This book is mostly about nongame birds.

The Department of Natural Resources keeps a special eye on hundreds of species of birds, animals, reptiles and amphibians in Michigan. Donations to the Nongame Fish and Wildlife Trust Fund through a special check-off on state income tax forms, helps the program conduct important research, habitat protections and other management efforts. Ask your parents to show their support for Michigan's endangered, threatened and nongame wildlife by purchasing a wildlife habitat license plate for their vehicle.

What's in a Name? Binomial Nomenclature

Some people call this bird a kestrel; some a sparrow hawk; and still others call it a killy hawk after its call, "killy, killy, killy." So, which is correct? In Michigan, the official common name of this small falcon is American Kestrel. But a species' common name can be different from place to place; especially if the people speak a different language.

Scientists saw the problem with common names and decided that each living thing needed a name that was exactly the same all over the world. They developed a system of scientific names called **binomial nomenclature** (by-no-me-all no-men-clay-chur).

American Kestrel

Whether you're in Muskegon or Madagascar, a bird's scientific name is always in the same language: **Latin**. Scientific names are written in italic, or slanted, letters. Each scientific name has two words. The first is always capitalized and is the genus, meaning the big group it belongs in. The second word is not capitalized and is the species. The American Kestrel's scientific name is *Falco sparverius*. Knowing this, you're well on your way to becoming a real scientist.

How to Watch Birds

We live in a big neighborhood! In Michigan, we share our land with wildlife neighbors that depend on us to treat them with respect and care. Here are some tips for successful wildlife watching and being a responsible next-door neighbor to wildlife.

To Find One, Be One!

Your best chance of spying on wildlife is by thinking like a bird.

MOVE SLOWLY AND BLEND IN

American Bittern

Sudden movements may startle wildlife. Take a lesson from the American Bittern, a bird found around shallow wetlands and lake edges. The bittern eats small prey such as crayfish, frogs and fish. It catches them by S-L-O-W-L-Y stalking along shorelines. The bittern's best moves are almost as slow as the hour hand on a clock. Bitterns also stand still, watching, until dinner swims a little too close . . . gotcha!

Just as moving slowly can help you see more birds, so can blending in. The bittern knows this, too. Its grass-colored feathers are a great disguise. Because part of being a successful wildlife detective is working unnoticed, it's smart to wear drab-colored clothing. Camouflage patterns that match your surroundings work great. Birds will be less likely to see you, and you may get a better look at them!

SHHH...BE QUIET, LIKE AN OWL IN FLIGHT

Some birds have very good ears. If you talk and make noise, they will hear you coming long before you see them. Great Horned Owls are super hunters partly because they keep quiet. Special feathers help them silently swoop down on mice and other small animals. When you're spying on birds, think like an owl and barely make a sound! Some birds also use their feet to feel the vibrations of your footsteps. Walk lightly if you want to spy a bird before it flies away with the wind.

KEEP YOUR DISTANCE

If you saw a giant watching you, would your legs feel shaky? Wildlife can feel like this if you get too close. Binoculars and spotting scopes can give you a close-up view from far away. If you're not using binoculars, hold your head still and move only your eyes. Animals do this to spy on YOU!

Using binoculars

LISTEN UP!

Bird calls, songs and other sounds can be hard to hear, especially at a distance. To improve your hearing, cup your hands behind your ears. It's amazing what you can hear now!

Wing marks on the snow

LOOK FOR CLUES

If you don't see any birds right away, look for signs they've been in the neighborhood. These include clues such as wood chips scattered around the base of a tree, holes pecked in a soft or decayed tree, droppings, food scraps and empty seed shells, wing marks on the snow, even a stray feather.

FEEDING TIPS

It's fun to feed birds in your backyard. Check the **Today's Special** listing for each species to learn what each bird likes to eat; some include tips on what to put in your backyard feeders.

Snap Photos Safely

Wild birds and animals can be unpredictable. They sometimes move fast, often without you knowing ahead of time. Keep a safe distance away. Many cameras have a zoom lens that allows you to get close-up photos while staying a safe distance away.

You may need to remind the adults with you about this safety tip. If your Mom or Dad thinks it would be cute to have a photo of you standing next to a moose or a Canada Goose, tell them to use the zoom lens and leave you out of the picture.

Souvenir Shopping

Souvenirs help us remember fun times. A photograph, drawing, artwork and your own stories are super souvenirs of time afield. Leave everything else in the outdoor neighborhood—including baby animals that look like they're all alone. Resist the temptation to "rescue" them. Chances are, their parents are nearby.

Look But Don't Touch

Your pet hamster may enjoy being picked up, but wild animals do not. Don't try to pet or touch a wild bird or animal; it may get scared and bite, peck or scratch you. Keep your distance, especially during nesting season.

If you really want to give wildlife a "hug," build a birdhouse or backyard feeder. Leave our big Michigan neighborhood the way it was when you found it. Then give yourself a pat on the back for being a responsible wildlife neighbor.

When to Watch Birds

Day, night, summer, winter. **When is the best time to spy on birds?**
  Look for the **clues**.

Birds Move When they are the least likely to be seen and caught by a predator; their food
  is available; they need the most energy and refueling; and when they need to, according to
  the changing seasons.

DAYTIME = DIURNAL

Birds that are active in the day and sleep at night are called diurnal. Why daytime?
Think like the bird. For example, hummingbirds are active in the day because the
flowers that hold the nectar they need only open in sunlight.

TWILIGHT = CREPUSCULAR

Many animals can be best watched at dawn (when the sun is just coming up) and at
dusk (when the sun is going down). Why dawn and dusk? There is enough light for
the animals to see where they need to go, but not enough for some predators to hunt
them. At twilight they appear like faint shadows.

NIGHTTIME = NOCTURNAL

Birds that are active at night and sleep during the day are called nocturnal. These
animals have special adaptations for being up all night. Owls have excellent hearing
and special nighttime and daytime vision.

Journaling and Phenology

Phenology is the study of the seasonal changes and
movements of nature. The return of the first robin
in spring; the migration of monarch butterflies; the
first and last snow of the year; and the first ground
squirrel you spy after winter hibernation, are all
part of Michigan phenology. Wildlife biologists and
ornithologists use phenology records to help them
understand the needs and behaviors of birds.

You can be a part of Michigan's ongoing wildlife
studies by keeping a journal. It's as simple as
writing in a notebook or on a calendar. Get started
with the journal section beginning on page 186.
Journals are fun to look back on. Plus, your
addition to Michigan's record might one day help
scientific research!

Seasons

Understanding how the changing seasons affect Michigan's birds will bring you wildlife watching success.

SPRING

Once the ice leaves the lakes, usually in mid-March, listen and watch overhead for returning birds. Look for waterfowl, hawks and blackbirds to lead the way. Shorebirds arrive in May. Warblers arrive in mid-May to late May. Birds are busy in the spring, finding a date and a mate. This is when males defend their territory, sing and do all kinds of tricks to attract a female or two. It's a very entertaining time of year!

SUMMER

Summer Gross Factor On hot summer days, some birds excrete waste down their legs to help cool themselves through evaporation. Gross, but cool!

In summer, birds are busy breeding (mating), nesting and raising their young. Shhh...by mid-July it quiets down. In some species, males leave the nesting area in late July or early August for a quiet place where they molt (shed) their bright breeding feathers and grow in duller colored plumage. They are ready for flight in time for migration.

FALL

By August, Canadian birds begin to pass through on their migration south. They are joined by some Michigan birds. Many species begin to group up in large migratory flocks and feed heavily in preparation for migration.

WINTER

In Michigan, winter means cold. Birds that stick around have slick strategies for dealing with the cold, snow and changes in food supply.

To beat the cold, birds grow an extra layer of feathers for the winter, like putting on a winter coat. Some will also fluff out their feathers to create more air pockets, which trap heat close to their bodies. Others lower their body temperatures at night to reduce the amount of energy (and food) needed to keep warm.

Another strategy is to make a group huddle—there's warmth in numbers! And some birds sit on their legs, or tuck a leg and foot, one at a time, into their warm body feathers.

How do the tiny legs of chickadees keep from freezing in the winter? Instead of having their veins and arteries separated by muscle like we do, theirs are side by side in their legs. The warm blood coming from their heart is right next to the cool blood flowing back to it from their legs. Heat exchanges between them!

Speaking of legs, some birds grow extra feathers around their legs and feet, or extra scales on the outside edge of their feet, for use as snowshoes to stay on top of deep snow!

Because food supplies often run low in winter, some bird species store food in bark cracks, crevices and tree cavities. Others bulk up (gain fat) in the fall in preparation for the extra energy demands of winter, while some bulk up before night and refuel the next day.

Because there is less competition for nest sites and food, some hardy birds may take advantage of the situation and begin nesting in winter.

Migration

FLIGHT PLANS: MICHIGAN'S FIVE MIGRATORY PATTERNS

Boreal migrants live in Canada but come south into Michigan when their northern food supply is short.

Permanent residents are birds that stick it out and stay in Michigan all year.

Short-distance migrants go just far enough south to avoid the extreme temperatures of our Michigan winters and return to breed in the spring. They travel to wintering grounds located from Iowa to Texas and Florida.

Mid-distance migrants breed in (or north of) Michigan and migrate to wintering areas in Central America.

Long-distance migrants breed here, but migrate to wintering areas in South America. These migrants travel up to 7,000 miles on their way from Michigan to their wintering grounds.

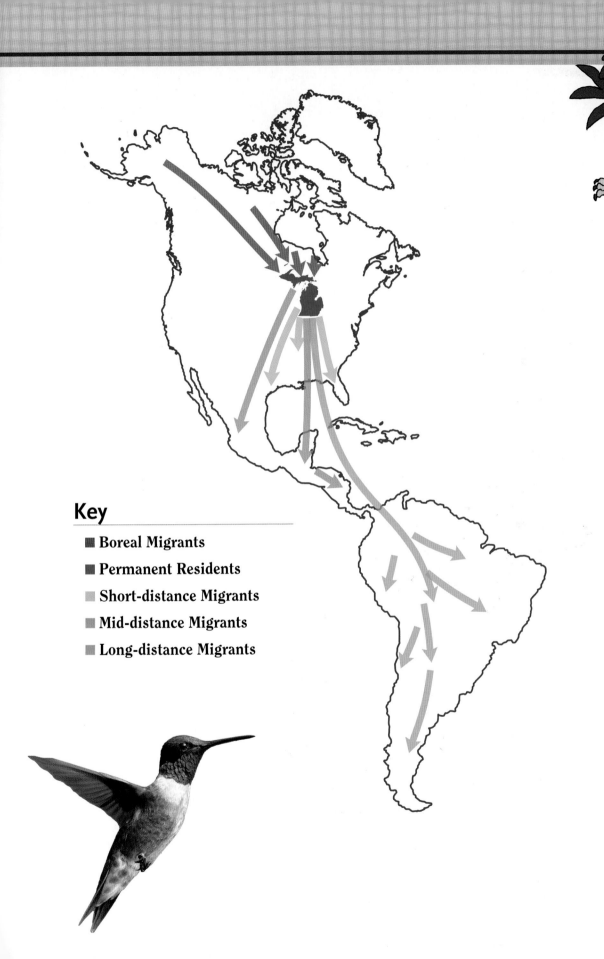

Key

- Boreal Migrants
- Permanent Residents
- Short-distance Migrants
- Mid-distance Migrants
- Long-distance Migrants

Where to Watch Birds

Make bird identification easy on yourself. Narrow down the possibilities by first knowing the habitat. After all, it is of little use looking for a water bird like a Common Loon on a prairie, or a prairie bird like a Sharp-tailed Grouse on a lake!

Michigan Habitats

Have you noticed that some wild places look different than others? Some have a few trees and a lot of grass, others are covered with trees, and some are a mixture of trees, shrubs and grass. That is because Michigan has different types of ecological systems, or habitats, and there are many different kinds of trees, shrubs and grasses within these habitats.

FANTASTIC FOUR

Michigan has four main kinds of habitats: coniferous and mixed forests, deciduous forests, open grasslands and prairie and wet areas. In each of these habitats, a combination of the climate (weather and seasons), geography, land history and soil support different kinds of wild plants and animals.

Before European settlement, the forest and prairie habitats closely followed the land regions on the pre-settlement vegetation map, and wetlands were found statewide. Because people have altered the landscape since then, we now have a mixture of habitats across the state.

To make identifying bird habitats easier, *Wild About Michigan Birds* is divided into four main sections: Coniferous and Mixed Forests; Deciduous Forest; Prairie and Open Grasslands; and Wetlands, Lakes, Rivers and Shores. The 70 birds in this book appear in the habitat section where you are most likely to see them. Of course, many can live in more than one habitat. Some birds are able to live almost anywhere. We have called these species, "Super Adaptors." Can you find birds in all four of Michigan's land regions?

Michigan has four major land regions. The area highlighted in dark green once supported primarily coniferous trees and light green, mixed forests. Deciduous (red) and prairie (yellow) were the dominant habitats in the other two regions. Wet areas are found throughout the state.

HIGHS AND LOWS

Most birds are more often found—or easier to see—at different levels in their habitat. For example, you're more likely to see a Wild Turkey strutting across the forest floor than soaring through the air. But just the opposite is true if you're looking for a Cooper's Hawk. To help you know where to look, a large picture at the beginning of each section shows the habitat. Silhouettes of each bird species are placed within it where you're most likely to see them, particularly during the day.

The silhouettes don't always indicate where a bird spends most of its time. Some show where the bird is easiest to see. Ring-necked Pheasants can be tough to spot when they are on the ground, tucked in grasses and other cover. But they're hard to miss when they fly to escape a predator, or hustle from a feeding area to their evening roost.

Check Off the Coniferous Birds You See!

When you spot coniferous birds, use these pages to check them off. The locations of these illustrations indicate where you might see them.

- ☐ Ruby-throated Hummingbird (pg. 30)
- ☐ Golden-crowned Kinglet (pg. 32)
- ☐ Brown Creeper (pg. 34)
- ☐ Boreal Chickadee (pg. 36)
- ☐ Purple Finch (pg. 38)
- ☐ Red-breasted Nuthatch (pg. 40)
- ☐ White-throated Sparrow (pg. 42)
- ☐ Dark-eyed Junco (pg. 44)
- ☐ Evening Grosbeak (pg. 46)
- ☐ Yellow-bellied Sapsucker (pg. 40)
- ☐ Blue Jay (pg. 48)
- ☐ Gray Jay (pg. 50)
- ☐ Ruffed Grouse (pg. 54)
- ☐ Common Raven (pg. 40)
- ☐ Great Gray Owl (pg. 56)
- ☐ Snowy Owl (pg. 58)

28   29

Coniferous-Mixed Forest

Coniferous-Mixed

Deciduous

Prairie

Wetlands

21

Sample Page

Common Name
The name used most often in Michigan

Scientific Name
Universally identifiable, two-part name originating in Latin or Greek.

Size
Measurements from the bill tip to the tip of the tail and wing tip to wing tip.

Photo
Most large photos are of a male in breeding plumage.

Field Marks
Identifying characteristics including unique colors, feather patterns, and bill, wing, feet and tail shapes that help you distinguish one species from another.

Birdsong and Other Sounds
Information about calls, songs and other sounds the bird makes—and what they mean.

Eastern Bluebird

Sialia sialis

Length: 7 inches
Wingspan: 13 inches

females

Females are duller in colo than males

Short, stout bill slightly notched at the tip for catching insects

Male is sky blue above

Young look like females but are speckled, and have blue wings

Rusty-orange throat and breast

White belly

"Tury, cherwee, cheye-ley." Male loudly sings this song to claim his territory. The same song is sung softly to tell the female on the nest "Everything's O.K., dear."

Wildlife Hotel: Immediate Occupancy

Bluebirds need tree cavities for nesting. Some people view an aging tree as useless and cut it d An older tree or a rotting tree is a wildlife hotel complete with buffet dining, single occupancy or dominiums. In Michigan, folks teamed up and built bluebird nesting boxes and placed them a forest edges and open rural and suburban areas that bluebirds need for catching insects. Since the number of Eastern Bluebirds in Michigan has increased. You can become a part of this su story by planting and leaving valuable habitat, and building and monitoring your own bluebird ing boxes. Learn more from the Michigan Bluebird Society, www.michiganbluebirdsociety.org

80

Bird Facts
Interesting natural history information, bird watching manners and tips for success.

Habitat Café
What a bird eats, how much it needs and when the food is available.

Habitat Café

Yumm . . . bring an order of crickets, beetles, grasshoppers, ants, spiders, earthworms, snails and berries. Eastern Bluebirds are *omnivorous*. Put wiggly mealworms on the ground to invite a blue visitor. Most pet shops have mealworms.

SPRING, SUMMER, FALL MENU:
Lots of insects, some fruits and berries

WINTER MENU:
More fruits and berries than summer, but insects are still the main course

Life Cycle

EST The female builds the nest cup of grasses in a natural tree
avity made by other birds such as woodpeckers, in tops of rotten
nce posts and in nesting boxes.

EGGS About ½ inch long. The female incubates the clutch of 4–5 eggs for 12–14 days.

MOM! DAD! Altricial. The parents feed their young right after
e chicks are born until three weeks after they leave the nest.

ESTLING The gray downy chicks will begin to look like a female
male at about 1 ½ weeks of age. By then, their feathers have
own in and they leave the nest.

LEDGLING If you hear *Tu-a-wee*, near a nesting cavity or box you
ll kn.. that a young bluebird is leaving the nest to perch on a nearby
nb or .n cover. They also give this call when they are waiting for their
rents .o feed them.

JVEN ILE In one year, they are mature enough to nest.

Unsolved Mystery
Is global warming affecting the seasonal movement of birds that nest in Michigan? Are they returning earlier, leaving later or not leaving at all? Solving this mystery requires clues (records) from people all over Michigan. In recent years individuals that have kept journals with bluebird departure and return dates have noted some significant changes. Keep your records in the journal section, pages 188–189. Be a part of solving this global mystery!

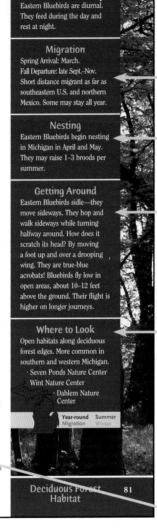

When
Eastern Bluebirds are diurnal. They feed during the day and rest at night.

Migration
Spring Arrival: March. Fall Departure: late Sept.–Nov. Short distance migrant as far as southeastern U.S. and northern Mexico. Some may stay all year.

Nesting
Eastern Bluebirds begin nesting in Michigan in April and May. They may raise 1–3 broods per summer.

Getting Around
Eastern Bluebirds sidle—they move sideways. They hop and walk sideways while turning halfway around. How does it scratch its head? By moving a foot up and over a drooping wing. They are true-blue acrobats! Bluebirds fly low in open areas, about 10–12 feet above the ground. Their flight is higher on longer journeys.

Where to Look
Open habitats along deciduous forest edges. More common in southern and western Michigan.
· Seven Ponds Nature Center
  Wint Nature Center
  · Dahlem Nature Center

Year-round	Summer
Migration	Winter

Deciduous Forest Habitat   81

When
Times when the bird is active. A bird can be active during the night (nocturnal), during the day (diurnal) or at twilight (crepuscular).

Migration
Does this bird migrate or stick around? If it migrates, look here to see when it arrives in spring, when it leaves in fall and where it spends the winter.

Nesting
When the bird starts nesting and lays its eggs.

Getting Around
Find out if this bird flies, hops, glides, dives, wades or soars.

Where to Look
A range map and notes offer tips on specific locations.
ELC=Environmental Learning Center
NC=Nature Center
NF=National Forest
NP=National Park
PK=Park
SF=State Forest
SNA=State Natural Area
SP=State Park
SR=State Riverway
SWA=State Wildlife Area
And if you spot any birds, write down here where you saw them and when.

History Hangout, Birding Tips, Do the Math, Did You Know? and Gross Factor.
Here the kids will find interesting facts, math questions, ideas for better bird watching and gross (but fun) bird facts. (The answers to the math questions are provided on pages 194-195.)

Life Cycle
Includes details about the entire lifespan of the bird, including nesting habits, information about the number and size of eggs each species lays, fun facts about what goes on in the nest and how nestlings and fledgling birds survive, the role of parents in a chick's early life, and the final stages of adolescence a bird goes through before becoming an adult.

Coniferous-Mixed Forest

The seeds of coniferous trees develop inside cones. Most of these trees are evergreen. Their leaves (needles) stay green and do not fall off every year. Why? Turn the pages to explore the coniferous forests of the north.

Land Before Time

Explore northern Michigan and find yourself standing on the exposed rock of the Canadian Shield, a layer of rock 2.5 billion years old! Colossal (very big) sheets of ice moved across the Michigan landscape over the past two million years, grinding down ancient mountains into mere hills and leaving behind giant rocks and glacial silt from northern Canada. Huge chunks of ice dropped off and made depressions in the earth's surface that eventually filled with water. The last of these glaciations, the Wisconsin Glacier, brought its own remarkable changes to the land 10,000 to 75,000 years ago. The actions of this powerful, mile-high sheet of ice paved the way for the coniferous, boreal and mixed forests of Michigan.

Tough Trees

Unlike the prairie, which nurtures plants with several feet of rich earth, northern glaciated areas of Michigan have patchy, shallow soils that are much lower in nutrients. The weather is extreme. To survive the harsh conditions, coniferous trees are well adapted to the short growing season, cold, heavy snowfall and shallow soils.

Coniferous Forest

Their shallow root systems draw nutrients (minerals) from the topsoil. A wax covering on their needles protects them from the extreme cold and winter winds.

The needles stay on all year. This saves energy and provides more time to turn sunlight and water into plant energy (photosynthesis). Conifers are tough, too: their branches can bend with heavy snowfall. Coniferous trees of the northern forest include red, white and jack pine, balsam fir, white cedar, white and black spruce and tamarack. Some deciduous trees have also adapted to the conditions and form the mixed deciduous-coniferous forests found across the Upper Peninsula and northern half of Lower Michigan. Deciduous trees of the mixed forests include aspen, birch, beech and maple. Five bird species that inhabit the mixed forests have been placed in the coniferous section of this book: Ruby-throated Hummingbird, Blue Jay, Yellow-bellied Sapsucker, Common Raven and Ruffed Grouse.

Michigan's Forest Wetlands

You can walk on a huge sponge when you venture onto one of Michigan's peat bogs. Formed in shallow basins left by glacial ice that later filled with rainwater, these bogs are a world of their own. The high acidity of the

Tamaracks in autumn yellow

peat (rich organic material of partly decayed plants), cool year-round temperatures, and the limited supply of oxygen due to poor water circulation, discourage bacteria and other decomposers from breaking down plant material. Over years, the plant matter builds up into a thick, floating mat of peat.

Plants that grow in the acidic, waterlogged peat have adapted to the conditions. Coniferous (cone-bearing) trees of a bog include black spruce, tamarack and northern white cedar. The needles of tamaracks turn bright yellow in autumn before falling off. This trait makes tamaracks a very unusual cone-bearing tree!

Be safe about bog-trotting. It is a good idea to venture onto a bog only with someone who knows the area. Visit a Michigan bog for a look at Boreal Chickadees, Red-breasted Nuthatches, White-throated Sparrows and Gray Jays. Prepare for a true north woods experience at Isle Royale National Park where most of the birds featured in this section can be found.

Winter Wonderland

You can explore the wilds of northern Michigan in the winter, too. It's a great time to learn how the hearty birds that live there year-round survive the cold, snow and changes to their food supply. Their adaptations to the cold climate are fantastic! White-throated Sparrows grow about 1,000 extra feathers in the winter for insulation and Boreal Chickadees huddle together in overnight groups for warmth. Turn to page 18 to learn more about how northern Michigan birds survive winter.

When the snow flies, take a clue from the local wildlife and dress in layers, wear warm boots or snowshoes, take along water and a snack for extra energy, and buddy-up with a friend. When searching, look for wing marks in the snow, wood chips scattered from a woodpecker's hole drilling, snow crystals outlining a grouse burrow and follow the tracks in the snow that tell a story. Be adventurous and, of course, always be safe!

Check Off the Coniferous Birds You See!

When you spot birds of the coniferous-mixed forest, use these pages to check them off. The locations of these illustrations indicate where you might see them.

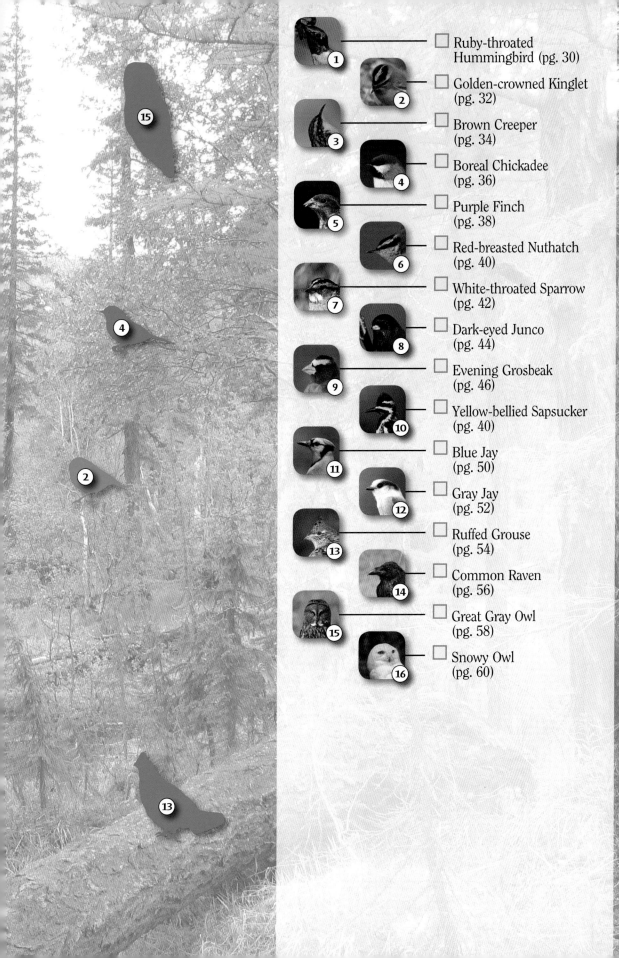

1 Ruby-throated Hummingbird (pg. 30)
2 Golden-crowned Kinglet (pg. 32)
3 Brown Creeper (pg. 34)
4 Boreal Chickadee (pg. 36)
5 Purple Finch (pg. 38)
6 Red-breasted Nuthatch (pg. 40)
7 White-throated Sparrow (pg. 42)
8 Dark-eyed Junco (pg. 44)
9 Evening Grosbeak (pg. 46)
10 Yellow-bellied Sapsucker (pg. 40)
11 Blue Jay (pg. 50)
12 Gray Jay (pg. 52)
13 Ruffed Grouse (pg. 54)
14 Common Raven (pg. 56)
15 Great Gray Owl (pg. 58)
16 Snowy Owl (pg. 60)

Ruby-throated Hummingbird

Archilochus colubris

Length: 3–3½ inches
Wingspan: 4½ inches

female

Females have a
white throat

Iridescent
green back

Male has ruby
red throat

Stiff, narrow wings
rotate in their sockets.
Large muscles power
a fast figure eight
movement.

Light gray-white belly
and breast

Its wings make a bumblebee-like humming sound in flight, and it communicates with quiet twitters and chatters

Michigan's Smallest Bird

Small bird—big appetite. Hummingbirds have the highest energy output per unit of weight of any living warm-blooded animal. What does this mean? For such a tiny bird, it uses a huge amount of energy. How does it supply this energy? It must feed every few minutes and survives the night with out food by lowering its body temperature and heart rate. To invite this tiny bird to your backyard plant tube-like flowers including Bee Balm (*Monarda*), cardinalflower, verbena and trumpetvine Include a nectar feeder. You can make nectar by boiling one cup of white sugar with four cups o water. Change the nectar often to keep your backyard hummingbirds healthy!

Habitat Café

Yumm . . . bring an order of nectar from up to 2,000 flowers per day, with a side order of insects and spiders. Ruby-throated Hummingbirds are omnivorous. Their tongue is longer than their bill, with a forked tip and grooves for the nectar to follow up the tongue like in a straw.

Today's Special

sugar water from nectar feeders

SPRING, SUMMER, FALL, WINTER MENU:

 Mostly nectar from flowers, with a few insects and spiders

Life Cycle

NEST The female builds the nearly 2-inch nest cup on a coniferous or deciduous tree twig, usually 15–25 feet above ground. She weaves plant down and bud scales to the limb with spider silk and disguises the outside with moss and lichens.

EGGS About ½ inch long. The female incubates the clutch of 2 eggs for 12–14 days.

MOM! DAD! Altricial. Mom raises the chicks, feeding them a mixture of regurgitated nectar and insects while hovering gently above.

NESTLING Chicks hear their mom's mew call and feel the air from her wing beats that signal it's time for lunch!

FLEDGLING Young leave the nest when they are about three weeks of age.

JUVENILE The teenagers become adults and are able to date, mate and raise their own young when they are 1–2 years old.

Do the Math

A hummingbird eats an average of 30 percent of its weight in nectar in one day! If you weigh 100 pounds, how many pounds of nectar would you need to eat each day? Do the math and put your answer here _____. (Check your answer on pages 194-195.) Just before their long migration, hummingbirds double their body mass by feeding on even more nectar and insects. Double your body weight—now how many pounds of nectar would you eat in one day? Do the math again. _____ Wow!

When

Ruby-throated Hummingbirds are diurnal, active during the day and resting at night.

Migration

Spring Arrival: May
Fall Departure: Aug–Sept
Long-distance migrant, wintering in Central America to Costa Rica. Some fly 480 miles on a 20-hour, nonstop flight across the Gulf of Mexico. On their spring return, they depend on Yellow-bellied Sapsuckers to drill holes that leak sap. This is their main menu until flowers bloom.

Nesting

Nesting begins in May–June in Michigan.

Getting Around

Masters of movement, they fly backward, forward, upside down and hover in one place. They are known to fly 60 miles per hour with up to 75 wing beats per second! Hummingbirds do not walk or hop—they use their small feet only for perching.

Where to Look

Areas with coniferous, deciduous or mixed forests, backyard flower gardens.
· Bengel Wildlife Center
· Estivant Pines Sanctuary

| Year-round | Summer |
| Migration | Winter |

Golden-crowned Kinglet

Regulus satrapa

Length: 4 inches
Wingspan: 7 inches

Males have a small yellow-orange king's crown with a black border

Females have a gold crown

Black eye line with white eyebrow

Wings have two white wing bars

Olive green above and pale gray below

"Tsooo-tsooo-tsooo-tsooo-
tsooo-tsooo-whip-lipalip!"
Male saying,
"This is my territory!"

Royalty in Miniature

Hone your detective skills and try to spy a Golden-crowned Kinglet in northern Michigan's spruce and fir forests. To succeed, think in miniature. These tiny birds eat tiny insects at the ends of branches and in bark cracks. Weighing no more than two pennies and barely the size of the end of a man's thumb, some kinglets stay all winter. The smaller the animal, the faster it cools. Kinglets maintain a body temperature about 3 °C higher than most birds, requiring even more heat-making fuel. To survive cold nights they feed heavily during the day to store energy, huddle in groups and may lower their evening body temperature!

Habitat Café

Yumm . . . bring an order of tiny, soft-bodied spiders, gnats, aphids, beetles, bugs and ants, with a side order of sap. Golden-crowned Kinglets are insectivores. Kinglets hop along conifer and shrub branches and even hang upside down to find insects at all levels of the forest, except the ground.

Today's Special

tiny spiders

SPRING, SUMMER, FALL MENU:
 Insects and insect eggs

WINTER MENU:
 Dormant insects

Life Cycle

NEST Both parents build the small, deep, sock-like nest 25–65 feet above the ground, hidden on the end of a spruce or balsam fir branch. They weave birch bark, mosses and lichens together with spider web silk and line it with animal fur and feathers. The nest is so narrow that the eggs are laid in layers.

 EGGS About ½ inch long. The female incubates the clutch of 5–11 eggs for 14–15 days. The large number of eggs offsets their short average life span of 2 years.

MOM! DAD! Altricial. Mom keeps the young safe by brooding them at shorter and shorter periods as they grow.

NESTLING Chicks are fed spiders and small insects by both parents.

FLEDGLING The stretchy nest expands to hold the growing chicks. There is a limit, and at about 18–19 days of age the chicks squeeze out of the nest pouch.

JUVENILES Golden-crowned Kinglets are mature enough to date, mate, nest and raise their own young the following spring.

Did You Know

Birds' bones are so light that their feathers may weigh more than all of the bones in their skeleton. This includes species that migrate long distances. In 1927, Charles Lindbergh, the first person to fly an airplane nonstop from New York to Paris, France, sat in a wicker chair and took with him only sandwiches, survival gear and two canteens of water to keep the weight low in his canvas-covered airplane. He even tore off the edges of his paper map to reduce weight. Keep it light for a fuel-efficient flight!

When

Diurnal. They are active during the day and rest at night.

Migration

Spring Arrival: mid March–April
Fall Departure: late Aug–Oct
Permanent resident to short distance migrant. Most migrate to milder temperatures in the central and southern US, but some kinglets winter in Michigan each year.

Nesting

Begin nesting in June in Michigan.

Getting Around

Nearly always in motion, they flit quickly and directly from branch to branch, jerking their wings in a nervous flight. To find insect prey, they search underneath leaves, twigs and small branches by hanging upside down.

Where to Look

Fir and spruce forests and bogs of northern Michigan and coniferous tree plantations in the state.
· Roscommon &
Delta Counties

| Year-round | Summer |
| Migration | Winter |

Brown Creeper

Certhia americana

Length: 5–5½ inches
Wingspan: 7–8 inches

hunting for insects

Whitish eyebrow above dark eye

Short legs keep the creeper close against the tree

Three front toes joined at the base for added support; long, sharp, curved claws give extra grip.

Females and males are brown with buff-white streaks, just like the tree bark they creep on. They are white below with a rusty colored rump.

Male and female look alike

Stiff, long tail feathers used as a brace

"Trees, trees, trees, see the trees." Males sing this territory song in spring and summer until the young chicks leave the hidden nest.

The Great Scavenger Hunt

The Brown Creeper scavenger-hunts for insects in the cracks of tree trunks. Finding the prize is a matter of direction—it creeps UP trees headfirst. Starting at the bottom of the trunk, a Brown Creeper climbs up, sometimes spiraling around the tree like a stripe around a candy cane. When it gets close to the top, it flies to the bottom of a nearby tree to begin its hunt again. Another hunter—the nuthatch—goes DOWN trees headfirst to find insects. These different views give both species a good chance of finding insects missed by the other. This makes winners out of both players. Teamwork.

Habitat Café

Yumm . . . bring an order of ants, caterpillars, insect eggs and larvae, moths, beetles and spiders. Brown Creepers are insectivores. Their long, thin, down-curved bill gleans (picks up) insects from tree bark cracks.

SPRING, SUMMER, FALL MENU:

 Mostly insects, some seeds

WINTER MENU:

 More seeds than summer, but still mostly insects

Today's Special

peanut butter and suet

Life Cycle

NEST With spider webs, the female attaches twigs, leaves and shreds of bark to make a hammock-like nest behind a loose piece of bark on the side of a dead or dying tree. The inner nest cup is lined with fine bark shreds and moss to keep the eggs and chicks warm.

EGGS Slightly longer than ½ inch. The female incubates the clutch of 5–6 eggs for 14–15 days.

MOM! DAD! Altricial. Mom broods the chicks for the first 10 days. Both parents feed the chicks and do their part in chick diaper duty from the time the chicks hatch until they are 5–6 weeks of age.

NESTLING Bad feather day! The chicks are born with a very funny feather-style. They have absolutely no feathers except for some gray down arranged in rows just above both their eyes!

FLEDGLING They leave the nest at age 1½ weeks of age. At night the young come together in a circle, with heads facing inward and the feathers on their necks and shoulders fluffed out.

JUVENILE At one year old, the birds are mature enough to date, mate, nest and raise their own young.

Birding Tip

Take a trip to one of northern Michigan's nature centers and wild outdoor areas to look for Brown Creepers. Explore Chippewa Nature Center for a visit with the small northern insect eater. See pages 196-197 for a listing of more nature centers. Don't forget your wildlife watching manners and plan for fun! In the meantime, set out suet, mealworms and smash peanut butter into tree bark cracks to invite them to your yard.

When

Diurnal. They feed during the day and rest at night.

Migration

Permanent resident to short-distance migrant, with some overwintering in Michigan. In September to November, they move to deciduous and wooded areas in towns and forested areas in warmer parts of the state. Others may migrate as far south as Illinois.

Nesting

Brown Creepers return to the northern coniferous forests in April. They begin nesting in May–June.

Getting Around

Parent creepers teach their young to act like a leaf and flatten out when danger is near. They make short flights from tree to tree when feeding. In keeping with their spiral pattern of foraging up a tree, the male and female fly around a tree when they perform their dating and mating dance.

Where to Look

Mature, old growth coniferous and mixed coniferous-deciduous forests, and timbered swamps with dead or dying nesting trees.
· Isle Royale National Park
· Chippewa NF

Year-round	Summer
Migration	Winter

Boreal Chickadee

Poecile hudsonica

Length: 5–5½ inches
Wingspan: 8 inches

Color varies from grayish brown to brownish gray

Brown cap and back

Females and males look the same

Rusty colored sides

"Pst-zee-zee-zee!" This soft song is sung up to 60 times per hour. When incubation starts, it drops to only 30.

Hide and Seek, Chickadee-style

Cold, it is very cold in northern Michigan in the winter. The weather changes often. To survive in the North Woods, Boreal Chickadees have become champion adaptors. For these tiny birds, having enough fuel to keep warm is a matter of hide and seek. Chickadees hide seeds and insects in the cracks of tree bark, branches and under needles in late summer and fall and then seek them when the weather is too cold or snowy for hunting. Before nightfall, they can gain 10 percent of their weight in body fat. They use this fatty fuel overnight and rebuild it again the next day. On a winter night, their body temperature drops as much as 20 degrees, using far less fuel to stay warm.

Habitat Café

Today's Special
peanut butter and suet
BIRD FEEDER TREAT

Yumm . . . bring an order of caterpillars, wasps, bees, ants, beetles, bugs, spiders and tree seeds—hemlock, fir, pine and spruce. Boreal Chickadees are omnivorous. Chickadees use spit, spider web silk or insect cocoon silk to hold a seed or insect in a hiding place.

SPRING, SUMMER, FALL MENU:
🐜 Lots of insects, some seeds

WINTER MENU:
🐜 Equal amounts of insects and seeds

Life Cycle

NEST The nest hole is made by another animal or made new by chickadees in the soft, rotten wood of a tree trunk. The female does most of the work, hammering wood chips loose and tossing or carrying them out. The nest hole is lined with moss and animal fur.

EGGS About ½ inch long. The female incubates the clutch of 6–7 eggs for 12–15 days. She eats the egg shells once the chicks have hatched. Yum, calcium.

MOM! DAD! Altricial. Both parents feed the newly hatched, blind and naked chicks. Delivering over 20 meals per hour can keep a parent bird very busy. For each meal there is a fecal sac (diaper) to carry away.

NESTLING The chicks grow white down and then full feathers.

FLEDGLING At 1½ weeks of age, they leave the nest and soon fly. Parents bring food to the chicks but in time the chicks feed themselves.

JUVENILE The teens leave the area of their parents to join a winter flock away from their parent's territory. They are ready to mate and raise their own young the following spring.

Did You Know?

Do Chickadees remember where they store their snacks? Research shows that during the fall, chickadees can produce new brain cells to handle the additional memory needed to recover the cached food in winter. They likely do not remember where every seed is hidden allowing other wildlife to benefit. In years when there is an outbreak of spruce budworms in the coniferous forest, more Boreal Chickadees are around. Foresters have a message for these worm-eaters: Thank you!

When
Diurnal. They feed during the day and rest at night.

Migration
Permanent resident. During the summer breeding season, they are in pairs, nesting and raising young. The rest of the year they flock together.

Nesting
Nest in the coniferous forests of the north beginning late May–June.

Getting Around
Boreal Chickadees hop from branch to branch and on the ground in search of insects. Short flights between trees are straight and quick. Look for the chickadee's tail to point up when it lands, making a V with its body. It quickly lowers its tail for balance.

Where to Look
Coniferous and boreal forests, spruce and tamarack bogs of northern Michigan.
· Tahquamenon Falls State Park

Year-round Summer
Migration Winter

Coniferous Forest Habitat

Purple Finch

Carpodacus purpureus

Length: 5–6 inches
Wingspan: 10 inches

female

Females do not have any red. They are gray with streaks of dark brown, a white eyebrow stripe and white belly. Young look like the female.

Crest can be raised, like a spiked feather-do

Back, head and throat are the color of raspberry fruit-drink

White belly and undertail

Notched tail

"Twitter-twee, twitter-twee!" Warbling song sung by males in late winter to spring to show off to females!

Eating Out of the Palm of Your Hand!

You can have Purple Finches and other birds eating out of your hand! Use materials from around the house and make a buddy bird feeder. Stuff old jeans, a long-sleeved shirt and old gloves with recycled papers. Make a head with a gourd or pumpkin using fruit on toothpicks for the eyes, nose and mouth. Get silly, put peanut butter or suet on top of an old hat. Lean your buddy against a tree or bush. Birds feel comfortable near cover. Fill an old baking pan or low basket with thistle, sunflower and millet seeds. Place it on the buddy's lap. In time, birds will get used to the buddy. You can then sit quietly beside it. Next, put the seeds in your lap and the hat on your head. Birds may snack on you!

Habitat Café

Today's Special
willow catkins

Yumm . . . bring an order of beetles, bugs, caterpillars, spiders, grapes, box elder seeds, buds and blossoms of wild cherry and plum trees, and aspen and willow catkins. Purple Finches are omnivorous.

SPRING, SUMMER, FALL, MENU:
- Mostly seeds, buds and blossoms, some insects

WINTER MENU:
- Almost all seeds, a few insects

Life Cycle

NEST The female builds the tidy nest cup 5–60 feet above the ground hidden on a coniferous branch or in the fork of a small tree. She weaves grasses, twigs and bark strips into a shallow bowl and lines it with soft, fine grasses and rabbit, snowshoe hare or deer fur.

EGGS About ¾ inch long. The female incubates the clutch of 3–5 eggs for 12–14 days.

MOM! DAD! Altricial. Both Mom and Dad feed the chicks and remove the fecal sacs from the nest—diaper duty.

NESTLING Chicks are fed regurgitated (partly digested and spit back up) seeds. Finches are one of the few songbirds that feed seeds rather than insects to their young.

FLEDGLING The young have their feathers and can fly short distances when they leave the nest at about two weeks.

JUVENILE Teenagers are mature enough the following spring to date, mate, nest and raise their own young.

Birding Tip

Do birds need the extra seed from backyard bird feeders? Birds can generally survive without the extra food, but it comes in handy when they are fattening up for fall migration, recovering in the spring or feeding chicks. Long, cold winters can make finding food and water tough for birds that stay all year. Once you start providing food and water, keep it up so you can enjoy the birds. Bring these neighbors close enough to get to know them by name!

When
Diurnal. Active during the day and rests at night.

Migration
Permanent resident. During the summer, they nest in northern Michigan. By late September – October they begin to move south throughout the state, including backyard birdfeeders. This movement peaks again in April–May as they move back to the northern forests to nest.

Nesting
Nest mainly in the coniferous and mixed forests of the northern half of Michigan beginning in May–June.

Getting Around
Purple Finches hop and walk when on the ground. They flit from branch to branch in short flights. In long-distance travel they have an up-and-down, bouncing flight as they flap their wings and then fold them.

Where to Look
Coniferous and mixed coniferous-deciduous forests, and backyard winter bird feeders.
· Whitefish Point (migration)

Year-round Summer
Migration Winter

Red-breasted Nuthatch

Sitta canadensis

Length: 5–6 inches
Wingspan: 11 inches

female

Female wears a gray cap and gray eye-stripe. Red color below is pale.

Blue-gray above and red-cinnamon below

Male wears a black cap

Black eyes hidden in a black stripe; white eyebrow stripe.

Juveniles look like pale versions of adults

White chin

"Yank, yank!" Both male and female make this call.

Fancy Forest Footwork

Head up, head down, turn around . . . How does a Red-breasted Nuthatch perform this fancy footwork? It has specially designed feet and toes. The first toe (hallux) is pointed to the back and the other three toes are jointed at the base and pointed forward. Like a mountaineer uses a pick when climbing up or down a steep slope, a nuthatch uses its hallux (first toe). While one foot is being moved, the hallux on the other foot is mounted into tree bark like a pick for support. When you see this tree climber upside down and headfirst, be amazed, he/she is an experienced climber!

Habitat Café

Yumm . . . bring an order of forest insects and seeds. Red-breasted Nuthatches are insectivores and granivores (seed eaters). Fill your bird feeders with seeds and suet for these backyard visitors.

Today's Special

peanut butter topped with sunflower seeds
BIRD FEEDER TREAT

SPRING, SUMMER, FALL MENU:
 Mostly insects, some seeds

WINTER MENU:
 More seeds than summer, but still mostly insects

Life Cycle

NEST Both parents hollow out a hole in a soft branch or stub of a dead tree, 5–40 feet above the ground. They may recycle a woodpecker hole. This deep hole is built up with shredded bark, grass and leaves. Mom lines the nest with feathers, fur and moss and puts a mat of sticky tree sap around the hole.

EGGS Almost ¾ inch long. The female incubates the clutch of 4–7 eggs for 12 days.

MOM! DAD! Altricial. With gummy resin around the nest hole, parents do not enter the nest after the first week. Instead, the young open their beaks close to the entrance hole for food delivery. Chicks poke their little rumps out of the nest for fecal sac (diaper) pick-up.

NESTLING Just before the young leave the nest, Mom and Dad put clumps of mammal fur on the sticky resin of the entrance hole.

FLEDGLING They leave the nest at about three weeks of age.

JUVENILE They search out other teens to form flocks during winter months.

Gross Factor

What is that white stuff on your car window? Bird droppings. Three kinds of wastes leave a bird's body in one package. The dark part is the feces (food waste from the intestine). The white part includes urates and urine, two kinds of waste filtered from the blood by the kidneys. Birds have the ability to conserve water by making their urine concentrated and chalky rather than liquid. What kind of bird left the dropping? Berry- and seed-eaters may have purple or green droppings. Insect- or animal-eaters often have darker brown parts to their droppings. Gross.

When
Diurnal. They feed during the day and rest at night.

Migration
Permanent residents to short distance migrants that move around Michigan with the changing seasons. In fall, winter and early spring they move to wooded areas with the most food sources. Some may move to central and southern parts of the state. They return to the northern forests in the spring to nest.

Nesting
Nest mainly in the coniferous forests of the northern half of Michigan beginning in late April through June.

Getting Around
Zooming through the forests, this bird stops only to pick up a seed or insect. It wedges the seed in a tree bark crack and hacks it open with blows from its sharp bill. Zoooom, it is off again in its fast, short flight to another tree!

Where to Look
Coniferous and mixed coniferous-deciduous forests and backyard winter bird feeders.
· Great Lakes Islands
· Hartwick Pines State Park

Year-round   Summer
Migration   Winter

White-throated Sparrow

Zonotrichia albicollis

Length: 6–7 inches
Wingspan: 9 inches

tan striped

White line over the eye with a yellow spot between its eye and bill

Black and white or tan with white stripes over top of head

Brown back

The square white throat patch gives this bird its name

Females and males look the same

Gray underside

Juveniles are more dully colored than adults, and have no throat patch

"Old Sam Pea-body, Pea-body, Pea-body."
Translation:
"This is my space."

Color-coded Birds

Hold tight, these birds are color-coded by the stripes on top of their head. Why? It appears to determine which birds are more aggressive and defend their territory and which ones are homebodies and take care of the young ones. White stripes identify a strong territory defender. Tan stripes identify a homebody. How does this work? Males almost always pair up with an oppositely colored female. This ensures that one is home with the kids while the other is keeping out intruders. It doesn't make any difference which is the male or female. Females with white head stripes even sing the male territory song. Tan-striped females do not. Get out your binoculars—color-coded birds may be in the area.

Habitat Café

Yumm . . . bring an order caterpillars, ants, beetles, bugs, spiders, snails and fruit, berries and seeds of plants. White-throated Sparrows are omnivorous.

Today's Special
snails

SPRING, SUMMER, FALL MENU:
 Equal amounts of insects and seeds

WINTER MENU:
Lots of seeds, a few insects

Life Cycle

NEST The female builds the bulky nest cup within three feet of the ground. Often, it is hidden in thick ferns, on a low tree branch, or a small bush. She weaves pine needles, grass, twigs, bark and moss together. The nest is lined with fine, soft grass and fur.

EGGS About ³/₄ inch long. The female incubates the clutch of 4–5 eggs for 11–14 days.

MOM! DAD! Altricial. Both parents feed protein-rich insects to the young. When the chicks turn with their backside to Mom and Dad, the parents take the hint and catch a fresh fecal sac (chick diaper).

NESTLING Parents shade the chicks from the sun and rain by standing over them and spreading their wings.

FLEDGLING The chicks are helpless, unable to walk or hop until they are one week of age. Then they leave the nest. At three weeks, they follow their parents, flying like moths around low branches.

JUVENILE On their spring return, they are mature enough to date, mate, nest and raise more White-throated Sparrows!

Birding Tip

Invite wildlife to your backyard. Provide what animals need: food, water, shelter and a place to nest and raise their young. Plant an American Mountain Ash tree and a Viburnum bush. White-throated Sparrows like to eat seeds and fruit. Scatter cracked corn, sunflower seed, peanut chips and safflower seeds on the ground under a bush or low tree. White-throated Sparrows live in the lower levels of the forest edges. Make your yard a welcome place for wildlife.

When

Diurnal. They are active during the day and rest at night.

Migration

Spring Arrival: April-May
Fall Departure: Sept.– late Oct. Short-distance migrant. Migrates in small flocks at night to the southern U.S. and northern Mexico. Migrating at night allows for calmer wind, fewer predators and the need for less water since they are out of the sun's heat. In fall and early spring they can be found all over the state.

Nesting

Sparrows nest in the coniferous forests of the north beginning in May.

Getting Around

White-throated Sparrows hop on the ground and through forest plants scratching the ground for food. They glean (pick up) insects from plants. They use quick wingbeats as they fly around tree branches.

Where to Look

Coniferous forests and bogs of northern Michigan. Prefers the undergrowth and forest edges.
· Seney NWF
· Pictured Rocks NL
· Ottawa NF, Davidsons Lakes
· Brandybrook
   Semiprivate Area

Year-round   Summer
Migration   Winter

Dark-eyed Junco

Junco hyemalis

Length: 6–7 inches
Wingspan: 9–10 inches

Bill is pale
orange-pink

Males are dark
gray with a
white belly

female

Females look like males
but are duller with brown
back and sides

White outer tail feathers.
"Signal of white—a Junco
in flight"

"Hack" means "This is my
territory." Both males and
females give this defense
call in all seasons.

Zelda-like Battles

Watch your bird feeders for flocks of 10–20 Dark-eyed Juncos during their fall and spring migration. Pick
out the dominant head honcho of the flock. This male sleeks down his head and neck feathers, pushes
his neck out and leaps toward other males. The little guys give in or get pecked on the head. Ouch! When
two flocks meet, the head honchos may have a battle. The winner is decided in a "head dance." The two
males meet face-to-face with legs and heads stretched tall and bills pointed to the sky. Kew. Kew. Clawing
and using their bills as swords, they have a standoff, spreading their tails like peacocks. Watching this
could be better than a game of Zelda. (Game on!)

Habitat Café

Yumm . . . bring an order of grasshoppers, ants, beetles, caterpillars, spiders and weed seeds. Dark-eyed Juncos are omnivorous. Scatter white proso millet on the ground or snow. Watch for juncos!

SPRING MENU:
 More insects than seeds

SUMMER, FALL, WINTER MENU:
Mostly seeds, some insects

Today's Special

black oil sunflower seeds
BIRD FEEDER TREAT

Life Cycle

NEST The female builds the nest cup on the ground hidden in thick weeds or up to 8 feet above the ground in a tree or bush. She weaves grass, bark strips, moss and twigs together for the base of the nest cup. It is lined with fine grass, rootlets and mammal fur.

EGGS About ¾ inch long. The female incubates the clutch of 3–5 eggs for 12–13 days. Mom may help the chicks hatch by pulling the eggshell with her bill. She may eat the shell to help replace the calcium her body used to make the eggs. Eggshells also give her the needed calcium to make a second clutch of eggs.

MOM! DAD! Altricial. Both parents hunt for insects, take turns with diaper duty and defend the nest and young against predators.

FLEDGLING Young leave the nest when they are 1½ weeks of age. In another few weeks they can feed themselves and fly as well as an adult.

JUVENILE Youngsters look like adults but with more brown than gray. At one year of age, they are mature enough to date, mate and raise their own young.

Gross Factor

Keeping the nest clean is a chore for some songbird parents. Fortunately, chicks defecate (poop) in tidy bags called fecal sacs. Like disposable diapers, fecal sacs have a strong outside liner to hold the droppings. This liner is made up of edible sugars and proteins. The first few days, parents eat the fecal sacs! Does it make them sick? No. During the first days, the chicks do not produce harmful bacteria; once they do, Mom and Dad drop the diapers away from the nest.

When

Dark-eyed Juncos are diurnal. They feed during the day and rest at night.

Migration

Spring arrival: April–May Fall Departure: Sept.-Nov. Short-distance migrant. Juncos migrate at night low to the ground. In the fall, some move to areas in central and southern Michigan while others fly as far south as the Gulf of Mexico. In general, males winter farther north than females.

Nesting

Dark-eyed Juncos nest in the forests of northern Michigan during May–June. They raise 1–2 broods each year.

Getting Around

Juncos hop forward and sideways on the ground scratching and foraging for insects and seeds. They fly with steady, quick wing beats. When flying against the wind, Juncos stay close to the ground. When flying with the wind, they fly higher; this allows the wind to "blow" them along.

Where to Look

Northern coniferous forests during summer months.
· Copper Country Trail, Keweenaw

Year-round	Summer
Migration	Winter

Evening Grosbeak

Coccothraustes vespertinus

Length: 7–8 inches
Wingspan: 14 inches

female

Males has black cap
and yellow "eyebrow"

Females are dull gray with
yellow underneath, white
rump and white on their
black tail. Young look like
females with a grayish bill.

Yellow belly
and undertail

Black wings
and tail

"Clee—ip!"
Loud call heard when
a group of grosbeaks visit
a bird feeder.

Gross Factor of Another Kind

Gross means disgusting, icky. Gross can also mean big and bulky. This is the perfect way to tel
about the big, thick bill of the Evening Grosbeak. Why do they need such a big bill? It works like
pair of large, strong pliers to crack open hard seeds, including cherry pits. Grosbeaks toss the oute
cherry fruit that you would eat to the side and eat the soft food inside the hard pit. Each spring, th
outer yellow layer of their beak falls off, like a snake sheds its skin. A new green bill is a clue that th
Evening Grosbeak you are watching is an adult ready to open hard seeds. Crack!

Habitat Café

Yumm . . . bring an order of pine, fir, red cedar, elderberry and spruce tree seeds with a side order of caterpillars, spiders and beetles. Evening Grosbeaks are *omnivorous*. Their bird feeder favorites are safflower seeds, black oil sunflower seeds and peanuts.

SPRING, SUMMER, FALL, WINTER MENU:
Mostly seeds, some insects

Today's Special
spruce budworms

Life Cycle

NEST The female builds the loose nest cup 20–60 feet above the ground in spruce and northern white cedar swamps. She weaves together twigs with moss and lichens, lining the inside with rootlets.

EGGS About 1 inch long. The female incubates the clutch of 3–4 eggs for 12–14 days.

MOM! DAD! Altricial. Both parents feed the young by regurgitating (spitting back up) partially digested insect larvae.

NESTLING Starting after the first week, the young eat whole insects and soft seeds on their own.

FLEDGLING Young leave the nest when they are about two weeks of age. Mom and Dad stay around and will shell seeds from bird feeders for the kids.

JUVENILE The teens are adult-size and able to fly and feed on their own at 3 months of age.

History Hangout

In April of 1823 near Sault Ste. Marie, Michigan Territory, a young Ojibwe boy heard the strange call of a black and yellow bird that ate the seeds of trees and fruits. The bird was given the Ojibwe name *Pashcundamo* from *pashca-un*, meaning soft, fleshy vegetable. From this the native name "berry-breaker" was formed. In 1823, a U.S. agent recording land boundaries made note of a bird calling at sunset. Then, in 1825, ornithologist William Cooper named it Finch of the Evening. However, it calls both in the evening and the day.

When
Diurnal. They are active during the day and rest at night.

Migration
Permanent resident. Evening Grosbeaks stay in Michigan all year, moving from northern parts of the state in the summer to backyard bird feeders throughout the state during spring, fall and winter months.

Nesting
Evening Grosbeaks begin nesting in Michigan in May–June.

Getting Around
Birds that spend a lot of time in trees also hop when on the ground. Look for their side-by-side hopping track pattern as you explore the forest floor. Their flight is undulating (up and down).

Where to Look
Coniferous forests, mixed coniferous-deciduous forests and backyard bird feeders.
· Isle Royale National Park
· Hartwick Pines State Park

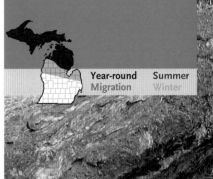

Year-round	Summer
Migration	Winter

Coniferous Forest Habitat

Yellow-bellied Sapsucker

Sphyrapicus varius

Length: 7–9 inches
Wingspan: 16 inches

Red forehead
and crown with
black border

Male: Red chin
and throat

Black bib on
upper breast

Female has white chin and
throat, may or may not have
red forehead markings.

Juvenile: similar to adult
except brownish on
head and breast and
faint head markings

Large white
wing patch

Yellowish
underparts

"Waa!" this is the call
given year round to signal
danger. Drumming mostly
by male to signal to female
and competing males.

Feathered Engineers

Who has been drilling holes in a nearly perfect circle around the trees? Yellow-bellied Sapsuckers drill neat lines of holes that leak a sweet sap that attracts insects. Sapsuckers then have a two-course meal, insects and sap! Sapsuckers are important members of the ecosystem, called a keystone species. Chipmunks, Red Squirrels, and House Wrens are just a few of the many wildlife species that use extra sapsucker nest holes. Golden-crowned Kinglets and Ruby-throated Hummingbirds depend on the sap for food when they return in the spring until flower nectar is available.

Today's Special

sap peppered with ants

Habitat Café

Yumm . . . bring an order of sap and ants with side orders of fresh fruit and tree bast (inner bark and cambium). Yellow-bellied Sapsuckers are omnivorous. They lap up sap with their brush-like tongue.

SPRING & FALL MENU:
Lots of sap with some fruit and insects

SUMMER MENU:
Insects with some sap and fruit

WINTER MENU:
Fruit with some sap and insects

Life Cycle

NEST Males arrive in breeding area a week before females to set up territory. They do most of the nest excavation using their bill as a chisel at a rate of 100–300 strikes per minute. Eggs are laid on the left over wood chips. The small entrance hole often causes parents to lose feathers going in and out. May reuse the nest hole for 6–7 years.

EGGS About 1½ inches long. 4–6 eggs incubated by both parents for 11 days.

MOM! DAD! Altricial. Both parents bring food to the young. During the first week, up to 15 trips per hour—one trip every four minutes! As the chicks grow, so does the size of the food prey. Most of the prey consists of soft-bodied insects with any large wings taken off.

NESTLING The chick closest to the nest entrance is the loudest and is fed first. After a few feedings another chick takes first place in the line-up for lunch.

FLEDGLING At about 4 weeks of age, they leave the nest.

JUVENILE Teens stay for one–two months drilling for sap. In fall they leave and join a winter flock away from their parent's territory.

Unsolved Mystery

Please pass the dip. When feeding young, parent sapsuckers gather ants and other insects and may then dip them in sap from a sap well. Does this provide extra nutritional value? Dip into this unsolved mystery!

When

Diurnal. They feed during the day and rest at night.

Migration
Arrival: April–May
Departure: Sept.–Oct.
Short to long distance migrant to southeastern US, Central America as far as Costa Rica. A few may overwinter in southern Michigan.

Nesting
Yellow-bellied Sapsuckers nest in Michigan in May–June.

Getting Around
Hitch (hop) up and down tree trunk, limbs, or when feeding on the ground. Watch for sapsuckers on aspen, birch, pine, spruce, hickory and maple trees. They have the best tasting sap in the forest.

Where to Look
Northern mixed coniferous-deciduous and deciduous forests. Their favorite trees include aspen/birch, maple, basswood, hickory and maple.
· North Country National Scenic Trail

| Year-round | Summer |
| Migration | Winter |

Blue Jay

Cyanocitta cristata

Length: 11–12 inches
Wingspan: 16 inches

raised crest

Blue crest

Black necklace, headband and eyeliner

Blue above and white below

Male and female look alike

White-tipped tail fanned out means the Blue Jay is about to land.

White wing bars

Blue tail with black bars and white tips

"Jaay, jaay!" in the Blue Jay's language means "Danger! Join the mob to chase it away!"

The Great Pretender

"Meow." Is this your pet cat, or is it a Blue Jay pretending to be a cat? Great pretenders, Blue Jays can mimic cats, hawks, screech-owls, American Crows, and American Kestrels. This comes in handy. Blue Jays have enemies. They do not like Great Horned Owls hanging around trying to pick them off for lunch. When a Great Horned Owl comes into the area, Blue Jays sound an alarm that mimics a bigger animal, like a hawk. The owl's cover is blown. One jay becomes a very loud and aggressive mob of jays, and they chase the intruder out of the area. No more owl on the prowl. Mission accomplished!

Habitat Café

Yumm . . . bring an order of insects, spiders, snails, tree frogs, apples, small fish and the eggs and chicks from nests—along with acorns, seeds and berries. Blue Jays are omnivorous.

SPRING, SUMMER, FALL MENU:
 Lots of plants, some animal matter

WINTER MENU:
 More animal matter than in spring, summer and fall, but still mostly plants

Today's Special

suet topped with peanuts
BIRD FEEDER TREAT

Life Cycle

NEST Both the male and female gather nest materials. The female builds the bulky nest cup 10–20 feet above the ground, hidden most often in a coniferous tree. She weaves bark, twigs, leaves and materials such as string, fabric and paper. The nest is lined with soft rootlets. The male brings her food while she works.

EGGS About 1 inch long. The female incubates the clutch of 4–5 eggs for 16–18 days.

MOM! DAD! Altricial. Dad does most of the feeding. Both parents hunt for food and remove fecal sacs (chick diapers).

NESTLING With eyes closed and no feathers when they hatch, the chicks have a lot of growing to do. By the end of the first week, their eyes are open and feathers are growing in. That is fast growth!

FLEDGLING The young leave the nest when they are about three weeks old and are able to run along the ground with fluttering hops.

JUVENILE Young Blue Jays resemble their parents but are a bit duller, grayer and browner in color. They are mature enough at one year of age to date, mate, nest and raise their own young.

Gross Factor

Do birds have flatulence (pass gas)? Blue Jays do. Adult Blue Jays were observed passing gas by a biologist who was studying them. Now you know even more about bird bodily functions. Word has it that they have a "hiccup" call too. Silly birds.

When

Diurnal. Blue Jays are active during the day and rest at night.

Migration

Permanent resident. Watch for groups of jays in Sept–Oct and again late April–June on the move looking for a tasty meal. To prepare for winter, they store acorns in the fall. A Blue Jay may store several thousand nuts or acorns each fall! This helps new oak trees to sprout, making Blue Jays an important part of the forest cycle.

Nesting

Blue Jays begin to nest in Michigan in May–early June.

Getting Around

Watch below the treetops for a Blue Jay to glide on its short, rounded wings with white-tipped tail fanned out—it's getting ready to land. During longer flights to gather acorns, as well as migration, Blue Jays fly above the treetops.

Where to Look

Blue Jays are *Super Adaptors!* They are found all over Michigan in coniferous-deciduous mixed forests, deciduous forests, backyards, forests, parks and even your school outdoor classroom.
· *Super Adaptor*

Year-round	Summer
Migration	Winter

Gray Jay

Perisoreus canadensis

Length: 11–13 inches
Wingspan: 18 inches

Short, black bill is used to twist and tug meat from a dead animal

No crest on head

Gray feathers camouflage the jay against the gray bark of a coniferous tree

Pale gray chest

Male and female look alike; juveniles are dark gray

"Koke-ke-keer!" This scolding call can be heard more than a quarter of a mile away.

Hiding the Loot

Have you ever saved your ABC (already been chewed) gum in a favorite spot for later? Then you and the Gray Jay have something in common. Gray Jays have a special throat pouch to carry food in and an extra large salivary (spit) gland. They stick their favorite food together with thick and sticky saliva and then glue it to a tree. If they think another jay has discovered their hiding spot, they will move the food to a different place and jam a piece of bark or lichen over it. When the snow blows and hunger hits, a frozen dinner is ready, allowing this robber bird to survive well in the harsh, cold winters of the north.

Habitat Café

Yumm . . . bring an order of butterflies, grasshoppers, beetles, bugs, spiders, ticks, mice, voles, the eggs and young of small birds, blueberries, mushrooms, soft seeds and dead animal meat. Gray Jays are omnivorous. They eat almost any small living thing in the northern forest.

SPRING, SUMMER, FALL, WINTER MENU:
Any available food item

Today's Special
suet, seeds and fruit
BIRD FEEDER TREAT

Life Cycle

NEST The female builds the bulky nest cup (8 inch diameter) hidden in the branches of a coniferous tree. It is usually 6–12 feet above the ground. Keep a hold of your tissues, they will hijack them and even cotton swabs for ultra-soft nest lining.

EGGS About 1⅛ inches long. The female incubates the clutch of 2–5 eggs for 16–18 days.

MOM! DAD! Altricial. Both parents feed the chicks and take turns removing the fecal sacs—chick diaper duty.

NESTLING Mom and Dad bring spit-covered "baby food" wads in their cheek pouches. Each glob of food is pushed out of their throats into the chick's gaping beak. The dark brown wads contain insects high in protein. Double yum!

FLEDGLING The young leave the nest at three weeks of age.

JUVENILE Teens stay in the area with their parents until June. The strongest bird chases its brothers and sisters away. When spring comes, Mom and Dad chase away this offspring and it is on its own.

Did You Know

When you spy a moose, take a close look for a Gray Jay giving it a free cleaning. Jays eat ticks from the moose's hide. There's a black fly . . . gulp. They catch annoying black flies from an antler perch also. Tasty little morsels.

When

Gray Jays are diurnal. They feed by day and rest at night.

Migration

Permanent resident. They tend to stay in their home territory year-after-year during all four seasons.

Nesting

Gray Jays nest in the coniferous forest of northern Michigan as early as March. An early nesting season gives young Gray Jays time to mature and learn the skills of food caching before the cold winter begins.

Getting Around

Gray Jays are skilled at sneaking up! They perch near prey and scout out the scene (including the baked beans on your picnic plate). Before you know they're even around, they glide on quiet wings, pick up the loot with their bill, and transfer it to their feet for a quick getaway. These antics have earned Gray Jays the nickname "Camp Robber."

Where to Look

Coniferous and boreal forests, spruce and tamarack bogs of northern Michigan.
· Pictured Rocks National Lakeshore
· Isle Royale National Park

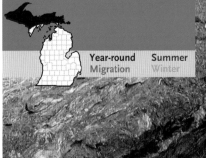

Year-round	Summer
Migration	Winter

Ruffed Grouse

Bonasa umbellus

Length: 15–19 inches
Wingspan: 22 inches

Ruff and comb feathers are fanned out when drumming or threatened

Males are brown, gray or rust above with streaks of white

drumming

female

Females look like males but tail bands are not as clear. Tail, crest and ruff are shorter.

Male has two or more white dots on rump feathers; female has on dot. Male's banded brown tail is fanned when drumming.

There are up to 50 wing beats in one 10-second drum . . . drum . . . drum roll.

Let It Snow . . .

How do grouse stay warm in Michigan's frigid winters?—They pull up a blanket and snuggle in—a blanket of snow. Snow is one of nature's best insulators, with tiny pockets of air that trap the heat of the grouse like a blanket. Watch out for snow-plowing grouse as they fly into soft snow from a tree, making an invisible burrow that is both warm and safe from predators. Getting around on top of snow requires a change in footwear. Each fall, grouse grow scale-like fringes on the sides of their feet that work like snowshoes. The extra width of the scales spreads their weight over a larger surface area, allowing the bird to walk on top of the snow. Put on your snowshoes and explore!

Habitat Café

Yumm . . . bring an order of aspen and poplar buds and twigs, leaves and seeds with a side of berries and other fruits during the summer. Ruffed Grouse are herbivores, but they feed only insects to their chicks.

Today's Special
aspen and poplar tree buds and twigs

SPRING, SUMMER, FALL MENU:
 Mostly seeds, some tree buds and twigs

WINTER MENU:
 Lots of tree buds and twigs, a few seeds

Life Cycle

NEST The female builds a simple nest on the ground at the base of a tree or under a large rock, log or tree root. The nest is lined with leaves, pine needles and a few grouse feathers.

EGGS About 1½ inches long. The female incubates the clutch of 9–12 eggs for 21–24 days.

MOM! DAD! Precocial. By late May–early June, the chicks are out of their eggs and on the run right away. Mom leads them to areas with insects for the first 12 weeks. She broods the chicks at night and during cold, wet weather until their bodies are able to make enough heat energy of their own.

The chicks add flying to their activities when they are 1½ weeks old. During the first two weeks, chicks eat insects that they catch on their own. By the time they are two months old, they eat mostly tree buds, fruit and seeds.

JUVENILE In late August and early September, they leave the family group and go their own way. Teens look like Mom, but without dark tail bands.

Do the Math

When the air is -27 degrees above the snow surface, it will be +24 degrees seven inches below the surface of the snow. How many degrees difference does the layer of snow cause? Do the math: ____ degrees difference. This is why a winter with little snow is actually unfavorable to grouse survival. Bring on the snow! Answer on pages 194–195.

When
Diurnal. They feed during the day and rest at night.

Migration
Permanent resident. Ruffed Grouse stay in Michigan all year.

Nesting
Ruffed Grouse start frequent drumming in early April and begin nesting in May in Michigan.

Getting Around
Ruffed Grouse walk on the ground and on the branches of trees and shrubs when foraging and feeding. Their flight is short with a quick burst of speed, followed by a glide to the ground, tree or shrub. Their short and rounded wings are made for fast takeoffs and turns around trees.

Where to Look
Deciduous and coniferous and mixed coniferous-deciduous forests with aspen trees.
- Barry State Game Area
- Hartwick Pines State Park
- Ottawa National Forest

Year-round	Summer
Migration	Winter

Common Raven

Corvus corax

Length: 24 inches
Wingspan: 5 feet

heavy, black
hooked bill

glossy black
feathers

shaggy throat
feathers

long, rounded wings
with separation
between flight
feathers

black legs

wedge-shaped
tail

"Rrock, rrock, rrock!"
is given by both males
and females declaring
their territory.

Voice mail, Raven-style

Calling all ravens—food! A raven sends loud voice mail to let other ravens know the location of food. It won't be long before they arrive. The announcement may also be made at the roost where locals and newcomers gather to exchange the neighborhood gossip. Ravens depend on larger predators like timber wolves to kill and open the body of large prey. Cars and trucks are partners in crime also. Early morning raven patrols along roadways may turn up fresh road-kill for breakfast. Ravens rip off pieces of meat with their hooked upper bill and hammer frozen meat with the sharp, pointed lower bill. They cache food in bite-sized pieces, each in a different location. "Rrock, rrock"—you have voice mail!

Habitat Café

Yumm . . . Bring an order of dead meat (carrion), eggs, insects, small mammals, grains, fruit, garbage. Common Ravens are omnivorous.

SPRING, SUMMER, FALL, WINTER MENU:
🦫 Animal matter and some grains

Today's Special
grasshoppers

Migration
Permanent resident in northern Michigan. Some wander into central parts of the state.

Nesting
Common Ravens begin nesting as early as February and into April in Michigan.

Getting Around
Ravens use deep wing beats. Look for the long fingers of the outer primary flight feathers. How does a raven dive? It tucks in both wings. Dive and turn? Tucks in only one wing. Watch for halfway rolls, full rolls and in a rare performance, a double-roll.

Where to Look
Coniferous, boreal and mixed forests of northern Michigan and central parts of the state.
· Porcupine Mountains Wilderness SP

Life Cycle

NEST The female does most of the work carrying sticks and constructing the 1 ½–5 foot diameter platform nest high (up to 98 feet) in a tree. The inner nest of smaller twigs and plants is made cozy with fur, shredded bark, grasses, sheep's wool and even paper. Nests may be reused in another year and can become very stinky.

EGGS The female incubates the clutch of 3–7 eggs for 20–25 days. The male feeds her and stands guard over the nest.

MOM! DAD! Altricial. Hatched naked with only a few gray downy feathers, the chicks look like tiny gremlins. The dinner call to the chicks is one short grunting sound from a parent just before it regurgitates into their open throats.

NESTLING Mom makes soft, comforting sounds and gently preens the feathers around the chicks' eyes with her large, thick bill.

FLEDGLING They leave the nest at 4–7 weeks of age when they can fly short distances.

JUVENILE They are mature enough at 2–4 years of age to raise their own young. Juvenile ravens may be seen "playing" tug-of-war, king-of-the-hill, sliding in snow and even hanging upside down!

Did You Know

A big black bird is overhead—is it a raven or a crow? Ravens are two times larger than crows and have a wedge-shaped tail. Crows have a square-ended tail. Ravens have a heavier, stronger bill with an angle on the top and shaggy throat feathers and wing 'fingers' too. Listen for the difference between the clear crow caw and the deep, hoarse rock of the raven. Raven or crow—now you know!

Year-round	Summer
Migration	Winter

Great Gray Owl

Strix nebulosa

Length: 22–23 inches
Wingspan: 4–5 feet

in flight

Yellow eyes and bill

Black chin with white bow tie

Females are generally larger than males

Male and female look alike

Take away the dense feather mass and this owl is taller but lighter than its northern cousin, the Snowy Owl

"Who-oo-oo-oo?" Listen for this deep call during the mating season, when male and female owls pair up.

Long 8–12-inch tail allows owls to move around trees to catch prey

I Hear You!

Finding food is a big deal to owls. To a Great Gray Owl, food means catching Meadow Voles. Look to the face of a Great Gray Owl for a clue to how they find small mammals. Their facial feathers are arranged like a satellite disk. This circular pattern funnels sound directly to their ears, located under the feathers on the outside edges of the disk. Your ears are the same height on each side of your head. The owl's ears are each at a different level. To know exactly where a Meadow Vole is in the grass or snow, the owl triangulates the sound. Never mind if the snow is deep and crusted. Great Gray Owls dive (called snow plunging) for small mammals and use their sharp talons to capture prey.

Habitat Café

Yumm . . . bring an order of Meadow Voles with a side order of mice, shrews, rabbits and snowshoe hares. This bird is a flying vole-trap. Great Gray Owls are carnivorous.

SPRING, SUMMER, FALL, WINTER MENU:

 Mainly voles, a few other mammals

Today's Special
juicy meadow voles

Life Cycle

NEST Only a few Great Gray Owls nest in Michigan. They do not build their own nest but recycle a hawk, eagle, raven or crow nest in the top of a tall tree. Not known to be skilled carpenters, the owls may repair an old nest with sticks and a new lining of feathers, dry grass and moss.

EGGS About 2 inches long. The female incubates the clutch of 1–9 eggs for 28–36 days.

MOM! DAD! Altricial. Both parents care for the young.

NESTLING The white chicks stay in the nest for up to three weeks.

FLEDGLING Once out of the nest, the young are cared for by both parents until they have their flight feathers, about two months old. Mom continues to feed them until they are 4–5 months of age.

JUVENILE Many teens migrate north to Canada. Both immature and adult Great Gray Owls roam except during the nesting-breeding season.

Do the Math

Once every 3–4 years the number of meadow voles drops very low in Canada, sending great gray owls south in search of food. Michigan experiences an invasion (high numbers) of great gray owls at these intervals. In the years following an invasion the number of owls can be half as high as the invasion year. This is called an "echo effect." Ask a Michigan DNR wildlife biologist for the year of the last great gray owl invasions. Then, plot them on the chart on page 194. Does a pattern form? Do the Math!

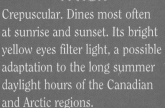

When
Crepuscular. Dines most often at sunrise and sunset. Its bright yellow eyes filter light, a possible adaptation to the long summer daylight hours of the Canadian and Arctic regions.

Migration
Boreal migrant. During hard, cold, snowy winters in Canada when food sources are hard to find they move south to Michigan's northern forests and nearby open areas to find food sometimes staying to nest.

Nesting
A few Great Gray Owls nest in the forests of northern Michigan beginning in mid-March–April.

Getting Around
Native Americans living in Alaska gave the Great Gray Owl the name "awkward walker" for its clumsy movements.

Where to Look
Coniferous forests of northern Michigan. Dense grassy areas of roadsides, fields and open coniferous/deciduous forest edges near a water source like a river, bog or stream. Low tree branches, signposts and poles along roadsides are popular lookouts.

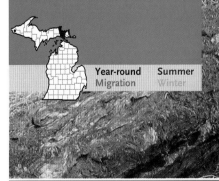

Year-round Migration   Summer   Winter

Coniferous Forest Habitat

59

Snowy Owl

Bubo scandiacus

Length: 21–26 inches
Wingspan: 4–5 feet

female

Females have heavy brown-gray bars across their wings and body

Large, yellow eyes

Blue-black, hooked bill

Males are pure white with a few dark spots on their body and wings

Long, broad wings

Immature owls are more heavily marked than females

Feathered, "insulated boots" keep the legs and feet warm. Shiny black talons.

The Ghosts of Winter

Winter ghosts come to Michigan on snow-white wings. They come from the arctic tundra (open, flat arctic plains) of Canada in search of food. In years with a bumper crop of lemmings to eat in Canada, Snowy Owls raise a large clutch of young owls and do not migrate south. In years when food is scarce, they raise fewer young and move south for the winter. Michigan does not have tundra, but watch in an open area for this owl, which can be mistaken for a large chunk of snow—look closer for the yellow eyes. Mind your wildlife watching manners and ask before entering private property.

Habitat Café

Today's Special
voles

Yumm ... bring an order of lemmings, rabbits, snowshoe hares, fish and carrion (dead animal meat). Snowy Owls are 100% carnivorous. Depending on their food supply, owls' lives can be feast or famine. When hunting is good, they can eat 1,600 lemmings in a single year; when times are tough, they can survive up to 40 days without food.

SPRING, SUMMER, FALL, WINTER MENU:
Lemmings, voles, rabbits, fish, carrion

Life Cycle

NEST The female scrapes out a nest in the frozen turf and moss in an open, windswept site. If the nesting area becomes drifted with snow, she may abandon the nest and eggs.

EGGS About 2¼ inches long. The female incubates the clutch of 3–7 eggs for 30–33 days. In years when prey is plentiful she may lay up to 11 eggs.

MOM! DAD! Semi-altricial. The chicks have a gray down that absorbs the heat of the sun and camouflages them from predators. They open their eyes on the fifth day. Dad brings dinner and Mom picks out the soft heart and liver to feed the chicks.

NESTLING The young are able to walk from the nest a two weeks of age but do not leave the nest for another couple weeks.

FLEDGLING Once out of the nest, Dad brings whole prey to the young. By the time the owlets are on their own, they have eaten over 1,500 lemmings! They can fly well at seven weeks of age.

JUVENILE It takes 2–5 years for the young to be mature enough to date, mate, nest and raise their own young.

History Hangout

Birds have been an important part of Michigan's cultural history. Our state is fortunate to host many cultural and historic areas including the Norton Mound Group, National Historic Landmark, Grand Rapids. Michigan is also home to many more historic trails, landmarks and sacred tribal areas. To learn more about the Native American Indians of Michigan visit, http://www.mi.nrcs.usda.gov/Indian.html.

When

Diurnal. They feed during the day and rest at night.

Migration

Boreal migrant. In years when they move into the northern part of the state, they are found from late October to late April. The peak is in November to December. Departure from Lower Michigan is by late March–early April.

Nesting

Snowy Owls do not nest in Michigan but move here from Canada for the winter when food is in short supply.

Getting Around

They perch in a spot where they can see all around and wait patiently for hours, listening for voles and lemmings under the snow. They swoop down over their prey and gulp—they eat small prey headfirst and whole.

Where to Look

Search flat, open fields and marshes in the southern and eastern Upper Peninsula. Look on open ice near and on Lake Superior and Lake Michigan's northern shores.
· Fish Point SWA
· Munuscong WMA
· Fletcher Plains

Year-round	Summer
Migration	Winter

Deciduous
Forest

Birds that live in and around deciduous forests have fascinating adaptations to one of the most diverse habitats in Michigan. Flight through trees that can outmaneuver a stunt plane . . . wood drilling to challenge the best of carpenters . . . songsters that can out-compose Beethoven . . . disguises that can fool the most clever detectives . . . and some of the most brilliant blues and reds found in nature.

On Again, Off Again

Deciduous trees lose all of their leaves every year and grow new ones. In Michigan, the species (kinds) of deciduous trees found in a forest depends on the land terrain (hilly, flat, etc.), soil type and climate. Deciduous forests are most commonly located in areas over Michigan's southern Lower Peninsula.

The maple-beech forests that once occupied large areas of southeast Michigan are fragmented into smaller tracts where Pileated Woodpeckers chisel in the trunks of mature trees in search of carpenter ants and Rose-breasted Grosbeaks chow on tree buds in the younger stands and at the forest edge.

Maple-Basswood Forest

Deciduous forests in Michigan's floodplains and swamps contain such giants as cottonwoods, silver maple and ash and these moist areas also contain sycamore, red maple and black willow. Eastern Screech-Owls search out tree-hole hideouts to perform their magic tricks.

The forests along Michigan's prairie and savanna remnants, open grasslands and fields host transitional (in-between) shrubs and plants that provide tasty fruits and berries. There are also large sturdy oaks that brace against the open winds with their broad outstretched limbs, dense wood and deep roots. The acorns of oak trees provide important year-round food for Blue Jays and Wild Turkeys. Watch also at forest openings for Red-tailed Hawks perched on tree lookouts.

The glaciers left a patchwork of soil types across Michigan. Major changes have also been made to the land over the past 170 years by forest harvesting, building development and agriculture. Because of these factors, you will often see a wide variety of trees and other plants living close together. This creates a diverse habitat for birds and other wildlife, so be ready for a wide variety of birds and animals!

Colorful Variety

More bird species live in a deciduous forest than on a prairie because there are more habitat levels in a forest. It's easier to learn about these bird if you explore the different forest levels.

Hawk Nest

The highest level, the top or upper canopy of trees, includes nests of sky dwellers like owls and hawks. Great Blue Herons (page 186) and Great Egrets (page 184), are water birds with long legs and feet adapted to both wading in shallow water and balancing on tree branches. They build their gangly nests in tops of deciduous trees in large colonies called rookeries.

Barred Owl

Birds that hunt for insects on tree leaves, branches and trunks use the middle level of the forest. So do birds that favor the seeds, fruit and nuts found there. Some birds nest in tree cavities. Others, like tiny carpenters, build nests in branches—some close to the trunk, others at the very tips.

Protective Camo, Amazing Antics

The ground level of the deciduous forest is home to birds that eat the seeds, nuts and fruit of woodland plants. Some birds prefer the snails, insects and worms found under leaves and in decaying wood.

Male Wild Turkey Strutting

Many of these birds are well camouflaged against the brown and light patterns of the forest floor. Their nests are built in grasses and leaves, under logs and even in structures that look more like a domed oven than a nest.

Turn the pages to learn about the birds that make their home in the different levels of Michigan's deciduous forests.

Take this book along on a walk in the woods with a buddy. For a long walk, you'll need an adult. Remember to tell a grown-up where you are going, who is with you and when you will be back. If your plans change, be certain to tell them right away. Safety first!

Check Off the Deciduous Birds You See!

When you spot deciduous birds, use these pages to check them off. The locations of these illustrations indicate where you might see them.

House Wren

Troglodytes aedon

Length: 4–5 inches
Wingspan: 6 inches

Fairly long, slender, down-curved bill for picking up insects

The young look like their parents

Short wings that are curved in on the underside

Males and females are brown above and light brown below

Narrow tail that is held up, down or fanned out depending on the signal

"Tsi, tsi, tsi, oodle-oodle-oodle-oodle." When the male's warbling song becomes shorter and quieter, it is a sure sign that the chicks have hatched.

Carpenter of the Forest

The pocket of a scarecrow's overalls, an overturned clay flowerpot, a boot left outside, a mailbox, an abandoned woodpecker hole, a deep crack in a rotten tree—all are used by House Wrens for a house. Watch wrens long enough and you can add to this remarkable list. Building and putting up backyard wren houses is the best invitation you can give to these small birds. Males prepare 2–7 houses for the female to choose from. Before she arrives, he is busy spring cleaning, bringing in furniture (small twigs) and setting out snacks (spider egg cases and larvae). How will you know which house is "Home Sweet Home?" When the female adds grass and feather pillows to her favorite cozy house.

Habitat Café

Yumm . . . bring an order of leafhoppers, grasshoppers, crickets, caterpillars, beetles, moths, ants, bugs and spiders. House Wrens are insectivores. The parents will eat snail shells for the grit and feed snail shells to their chicks for the calcium content.

SPRING, SUMMER, FALL, WINTER MENU:

 Almost entirely insects

Life Cycle

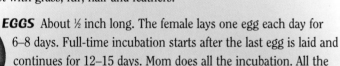

NEST The female finishes the nest started by the male and makes an average of 300 trips to the nest in only a few days. She lines the nest with grass, fur, hair and feathers.

EGGS About ½ inch long. The female lays one egg each day for 6–8 days. Full-time incubation starts after the last egg is laid and continues for 12–15 days. Mom does all the incubation. All the eggs hatch on the same day.

MOM! DAD! Altricial. At first, Dad "beaks" the insects over to Mom and she feeds the chicks. After the first days, they both feed the chicks, remove fecal sacs (diaper duty) and carry the sacs away from the nest.

NESTLING The downy chicks stay in the nest about two weeks.

FLEDGLING After leaving the nest the parents bring the kids insects for another two weeks.

JUVENILE In late August, wrens leave the shrubby nest site and prepare for migration in the safety of a more thickly forested area. On their spring return, they are mature enough to date, mate and set up house for their own young.

Did You Know

How do bird eggs stay warm? Incubating parents have a brood patch. This bare spot on the bird's belly has many blood vessels close to the skin's surface. During incubation, the blood flow to this area increases, making it a real "hot spot." The parent sits with the eggs directly under the brood patch. Once the parent's job of keeping eggs and chicks warm is finished, feathers regrow and the brood patch disappears.

When

House Wrens are diurnal. They feed during the day and rest at night.

Migration

Spring Arrival: late-April – May
Fall Departure: Sept – Oct
The House Wren is a short distance migrant to the southern U.S. and Mexico.

Nesting

In Michigan, House Wrens begin nesting in May. They raise 1–2 broods each year. Watch for wrens in your neighborhood, nest territories are ½ to ¾ of an acre in size, or an average city block.

Getting Around

House Wrens hop on the ground and fly from bush to bush in search of insects. Their longer flights are straight and steady. If a wren's tail is straight-up, the bird feels excited or in danger. Tail down means it is comfortable. A male with a fanned out and lowered tail, head held forward, and fluffed up back feathers, is defending his territory.

Where to Look

Open shrubby woodlands, habitat edges including backyards and parks all over Michigan.
· *Super Adaptor*

Year-round	Summer
Migration	Winter

Deciduous Forest Habitat

Indigo Bunting

Passerina cyanea

Length: 5–5½ inches
Wingspan: 8 inches

Black eyes

The male is deep blue in the breeding season; during the rest of the year, he is brown with a tan underside and a blue rump.

female

Females are pale brown with light wing bars

"Indigo" means "blue" but these buntings are actually brown. The blue color is light reflecting off the top layer of the feathers. The true brown-gray feather color can be seen when sunlight is not directly on the feathers.

Black legs

"Blue-blue, where-where, here-here, see-it, see-it." The male's spring and summer song. First-year males learn from a male next door.

Night Migration

How do Indigo Buntings know which direction to fly during night migration? Do they use the stars a. a map? To find an answer, scientists placed young birds in a planetarium (star theater) and expose them to the rotation of stars that occur in winter, spring, summer and fall. The birds turned to th north in the "spring" and to the south in the "fall." Were the stars the only clue to finding nort and south? Birds also turned north and south based on their hormones (body chemicals). Shifts i hormone levels were triggered by changes in the amount of daylight. Hormone levels may be wh some bird species start gaining and storing extra fat and get "restless" a few weeks before migration.

day's Special
white proso
millet
BIRD FEEDER TREAT

Habitat Café

Yumm . . . bring an order of grasshoppers, caterpillars, beetles, seeds and berries. Indigo Buntings are omnivorous.
They glean (pick up) insects from plants.

SPRING, SUMMER, FALL MENU:

Mainly insects, some seeds and berries

WINTER MENU:

Lots of seeds and buds, a few insects

Life Cycle

NEST The female builds a nest cup in the branches of a shrub just 1–3 feet above the ground. She weaves strips of bark, grass stems and leaves together. Spider webs are woven in and out to hold the grasses and leaves together. The inside is lined with fine grasses, rootlets, animal hair and fur.

EGGS About ½ inch long. The female incubates the clutch of 3–4 eggs for 11–12 days.

MOM! DAD! Altricial. Mom takes care of the chicks in this family. Dad is nearby calling out warnings to predators to stay far away.

NESTLING While Mom is out of the nest getting food, the young huddle together to stay warm and save energy.

FLEDGLING The young leave the nest when they are just over one week old.

JUVENILE Juvenile buntings flock together and prepare for fall migration. In the first year, young males may be brown or a brown-blue mix with white wing bars. During their first breeding season, male buntings learn the songs of other adult males in their territorial neighborhood.

Unsolved Mystery

Science is about solving mysteries. Using the same scientific method you use to do a science fair project, scientists pose a question and hypothesis, design experiments to test it and study the results (data). Did the results answer the question or provide clues? What is the conclusion? Scientists use the new information to make our world a better place to live. Detective work is waiting for you. Enter your school science fair and solve a mystery!

When

Indigo Buntings are diurnal. They feed during the day and rest at night.

Migration

Spring Arrival: May
Fall Departure: September
Long-distance migrant by night over the Gulf of Mexico to Central America and the Neotropics.

Nesting

Indigo Buntings begin nesting in late May. Record your nest records in Journal Pages (pp. 186–189).

Getting Around

Indigo Buntings hop from branch to branch and on the ground when searching for insects. Check the bottom of your shoes. Do they have treads that give you better grip when running? Birds need grip, too. Scales on the bottom of their feet allow them to grip tree branches, slippery rocks along lakeshores and more.

Where to Look

Brushy edges and woodland borders.
· Hiawatha National Forest
· Fort Custer Recreation Area

Year-round	Summer
Migration	Winter

Deciduous Forest Habitat   71

Black-capped Chickadee

Poecile atricapillus

Length: 5–6 inches
Wingspan: 8 inches

Short, small, black bill shaped like a cone

Black cap and chin

Weighs only as much as one quarter!

White breast and belly

Gray back

Females and males look the same

Long tail

"Chickadee-dee, Chickadee-dee-dee" means "Hey, I'm over here!" "Fee-bee, fee-bee" is often a male saying, "This is my space!"

A Tiny Bird With Mighty Adaptations

Michigan's deciduous forests are home to a tiny, yet mighty, survivor. The Black-capped Chickadee stays in Michigan all year. They have adapted to the cold, snowy winters by lowering their body temperature at night. This helps them use less energy so they can skip the extra trip for a midnight snack. During the day, chickadees fill up on high energy foods and stash snacks for later use. A Michigan hunter watched a group of chickadees each carry away about one pound of deer fat in a single day! They stuffed and pounded it with their small pointed bills into every tree bark hole and crack they could find. A mighty job for a tiny bird.

Habitat Café

Yumm . . . bring an order of caterpillars and the eggs of gypsy and codling moths. A friend of Michigan's forest, they eat moths that are destructive to some trees. Black-capped Chickadees are insectivores.

SPRING, SUMMER, FALL MENU:
 Mostly insects, some seeds and berries

WINTER MENU:
 Insects and an equal amount of seeds, berries and fat

day's Special

spiders

Life Cycle

NEST A hole is made in the soft, rotten wood of a tree, 4–10 feet above ground. The female lines the nest with rabbit fur, moss, feathers and even the soft threads of insect cocoons. A chickadee uses a different nest each year, whether it makes its own, uses one made by woodpeckers or a manmade nest box.

EGGS About ½ inch long. The female incubates 6–8 eggs for 12–13 days. The male brings food.

MOM! DAD! Altricial. Both Mom and Dad feed the young and remove the fecal sacs (chick diapers) covered in a slippery coating. This makes the job of taking them out of the nest much easier!

NESTLING The young leave the nest when they are just over two weeks old.

FLEDGLING Their pink feet and bill soon turn black and they look just like Mom and Dad.

JUVENILE Teens stay with their parents for about a month and then join a small winter flock. At one year of age, they are mature enough to date, mate, nest and raise their own young.

Birding Tips

When you slice a summer melon and carve an October pumpkin, save the seeds for backyard birds. First, spread the seeds on a pan to dry. Then, place the dry seeds on the ground or in a feeder. Birds need water too. Hang a milk jug with a tiny hole in the bottom above a birdbath or pool of water. Birds are attracted to the sound of dripping water.

When

Diurnal. Chickadees feed during the day and rest at night.

Migration

Permanent resident. In winter, chickadees form groups of 6–10 birds, breaking up into pairs in spring. On cold winter nights they may squeeze into their own small tree hollow or share a large tree cavity or roost box with up to 50 small birds.

Nesting

Chickadees begin excavating nest holes in April, with egg laying and incubation during May–June in Michigan.

Getting Around

Look for a flash of lighter color on the tips of their gray wings in flight. When they need to escape a predator they can change directions in just three-hundreths of a second! How do they stay hanging upside down while picking insects off the underside of a tree branch? They have special leg muscles. They creep up and down tree trunks and hop from twig to twig.

Where to Look

Deciduous and mixed forest with open edges all over Michigan.
· Backyard birdhouses and feeders

Year-round	Summer
Migration	Winter

Ovenbird

Seiurus aurocapilla

Length: 6 inches
Wingspan: 9–10 inches

orange cap

Rusty orange cap with a black rim

Brown on top

White eye-ring

White below with dark brown streaks

Male and female look alike

Pink legs and feet

"Teacher, teacher, teacher, teacher, teacher, teacher" is Ovenbird for "This is my space!"

Head Over Wing in Love

The Ovenbird has a mating song and dance worth trekking to Michigan's forest to watch in June and July. By the light of the sun or moon, the flirting male darts to the top of a tree. From there he dashes through the air in a series of hot-rod zigzags. Shifting speeds, he spreads his wings and coasts grace-fully to the forest floor while serenading his gal. Ovenbirds have likely been doing this head-over-wing dance for 10,000 years, at least. Will they be able to continue? Since the mid-1900s there are fewer and fewer Ovenbirds. Roads, houses, offices and farms break large forests into smaller pieces, called forest fragmentation. Ovenbirds need the deep inside of a forest to survive.

Habitat Café

Yumm . . . bring an order of grasshoppers, ants, beetles, bugs and small seeds. Mom eats the eggshells immediately after the chicks hatch! The shells are like a calcium vitamin to replace the calcium her body used to make the clutch of eggs. Ovenbirds are omnivorous. They eat both plant and animal matter.

SPRING, SUMMER, FALL, WINTER MENU:
Almost entirely insects, some seeds

oday's Special

earthworms

Life Cycle

NEST The female builds the domed nest beginning with a small hollow in the forest floor. Using dead leaves, grass, weed stems, rootlets and moss, she weaves a dome, or upside-down bowl, over the top. She includes a side entrance. On the inside she makes a cup nest with fine rootlets, animal hair, and fur.

EGGS About ⅝ inch long. The female incubates the clutch of 4–5 eggs for 11–14 days.

MOM! DAD! Altricial. Both parents feed insects to the young and do diaper duty by eating the fecal sacs. When young Ovenbirds are nearly ready to fledge, parents carry the fecal sacs away from the nest to deter predators. Bird diapers can be smelly!

NESTLING The gray, downy chicks stay in the nest for just over a week and then practice hopping.

FLEDGLING By three weeks of age, their feathers have grown in enough to begin flight lessons.

JUVENILE At this age, teens practice escaping from predators by playing tag. They fatten up on insects before their long migration south.

Birding Tips

How close is too close? You are minding your wildlife manners when your presence does not change an animal's behavior. If an animal does notice you, move slowly and quietly away. Make a wildlife watching blind in your backyard with things you already have at home, such as old sheets or a tent. Camouflage your hideout and learn about your wild neighbors!

When

Ovenbirds are diurnal, active during the day and resting at night.

Migration

Spring arrival: late April - May
Fall departure: Sept- Oct
Long-distance migrants. Ovenbirds migrate at night at heights of 500–1000 feet (the height of a 8–16 story building) on their migration flights to wintering areas in South America. How fast do they fly on these high flights? About 40 mph.

Nesting

Begins nesting in May in Michigan. The nest is so well camouflaged it is nearly invisible! It looks like a Dutch oven, which gives this bird its interesting name.

Getting Around

Ovenbirds walk on the ground and fly low to the ground. Watch for their tail to pump up and down when they fly from tree to tree.

Where to Look

Ovenbirds need areas of deciduous and mixed forests of at least 250 acres in size.
· Luzerne Boardwalk near Mio

Year-round   Summer
Migration   Winter

White-breasted Nuthatch

Sitta carolinensis

Length: 6 inches
Wingspan: 11 inches

female

Females have a blue-gray cap and black on back of neck (nape)

Young look like females

Blue-gray back

Rusty brown undertail

Males have a black cap

Short, very strong black legs for holding onto tree bark and branches

White breast

Long, slightly curved bill tapers to a point

"Yank, yank, yank" means "I'm over here!" Both males and females use this call to check in with each other.

Look out below! I'm coming down headfirst!

The White-breasted Nuthatch has a game plan for finding food. It has to. There are other bird species after the same insects. The White-breasted Nuthatch is a "hop down the tree headfirst insect gleaner." They also work their way up, sideways, while looking for food. Where do they store their groceries? They cache the food in tree bark cracks. Pounding a sunflower seed into a bark crack can open the seed for eating right away, or it can be covered with moss, rotten wood or snow for munching on later. A male nuthatch tried six different places in the bark and branches of a large maple tree to hide its yummy seed. It was hidden, except from this author (and wildlife detective)!

Habitat Café

Yumm . . . bring an order of grasshoppers, caterpillars, beetles, seeds and berries. White-breasted Nuthatches are omnivorous. Seeds provide fats and carbohydrates needed to refuel during winter months.

SPRING, SUMMER, FALL MENU:

 Equal amounts of insects and seeds

WINTER MENU:

 Mostly seeds and suet, fewer insects than during spring, summer and fall

day's Special

suet and
eanut butter
BIRD FEEDER TREAT

Life Cycle

NEST The female builds the nest 5–20 feet above the ground in a rotted out tree knot, tree cavity or even a nesting box. She brings in twigs and grasses for the nest base and lines it with fine grass, hair, fur, wool and feathers.

 EGGS About ½ inch long. The female incubates the clutch of 6–9 eggs for 11–12 days. The male enters the nesting hole only to feed the female.

MOM! DAD! Altricial. Mom and Dad make many trips for insects to feed their hungry brood. How many? Up to 22 trips per hour.

NESTLING The chicks stay in the nest for about one month. Parents keep squirrels out by sweeping the nest with an insect (a beetle) that leaks sticky, oily fluid from its crushed legs! They may also sway back and forth with wings spread to surprise a squirrel into hightailing it down the tree.

FLEDGLING The young birds stay with Mom and Dad for another few weeks after they leave the nest.

JUVENILE Juveniles leave their parents' territory to find their own space.

Birding Tip

Mealworms for dinner! Birds that stay in Michigan during the winter need protein to keep up their heat-making energy. Take a trip to your local bird, pet or fishing bait shop and stock up on mealworms. Simply keep them in the refrigerator, but clue your parents in or worms may make a surprise pizza topping. Place the worms in a flat bird feeder and watch for nuthatches, chicka-dees, cardinals, juncos and woodpeckers to chow down. Tasty!

When

White-breasted Nuthatches are diurnal. They feed during the day and rest at night.

Migration

Permanent resident. They stay all year and use their energy to find insects in the less crowded winter forest. Birds that migrate use their energy to make the long round-trip.

Nesting

Begin nesting in April–May in Michigan. Prefer nest sites near edges of woodlands.

Getting Around

Nuthatches use their long, somewhat pointed wings for quick darting flights from tree to tree. Because they have a short tail, they spread their feet far apart and at a slight angle from the tree bark for support while feeding. Watch them pick up a seed, fly off to a tree trunk, then hide the tidbit for a later snack.

Where to Look

Deciduous forests throughout Michigan with fewer in the Upper Peninsula. Backyard trees, bird feeders, parks, orchards and farm lots with mature trees.

- Hartwick Pines State Park
- South Higgins Lake State Park

Year-round	Summer
Migration	Winter

Deciduous Forest Habitat

Downy Woodpecker

Picoides pubescens

Length: 6–7 inches
Wingspan: 12 inches

Males have red
patch on nape
(back of neck)

female

Females do not have red
on nape (back of neck)

White belly

White stripe down
the back

Young male has a
red spot on top of
his head

Black with white
spotted wings

Black spots on
white tail feathers

"Drum, drum"
is rapped on
dry limbs.

Built for the Job

The Downy Woodpecker is the smallest woodpecker in Michigan and the most common. It is built to survive and can balance on weed stems and small branches, unlike larger members of the woodpecker family. Look for this black and white wonder balanced on the stems of goldenrod plants. It is most likely pecking wasp larvae from inside their cozy gall home. Using its strong bill, long, barbed tongue (up to four times the length of its bill) and sticky spit, Downy Woodpeckers rake in insects from cracks and tunnels. Where does it store its long tongue? Curled inside its head like a tape measure!

Habitat Café

Yumm . . . bring an order of crickets, wasps, grasshoppers, ants, beetles, flies, spiders, acorns, berries and fruit. Downy Woodpeckers are omnivorous. Fill your feeders with suet, peanut butter and nuts.

SPRING, SUMMER, FALL, WINTER MENU:
Lots of insect larvae, some seeds

day's Special
sect larvae in
Idenrod galls

Life Cycle

NEST The female and male make the nesting hole in a tree, fence post or tree stump 3–50 feet above the ground. The hole is 1¼ inches in diameter and 8–12 inches deep. They will use a birdhouse for roosting but not usually for nesting.

EGGS About ½ inch long. Both the male and female incubate the clutch of 4–5 eggs for 11–12 days.

MOM! DAD! Altricial. Mom and Dad put small, soft insects directly into the helpless chicks' open bills.

NESTLING When the young birds are just over a week old, they climb to the top of the nest cavity to be fed. Woodpecker chicks have a heel pad that protects their feet from the rough nest edges. The pad is shed once they leave the nest.

FLEDGLING The young birds can fly and leave the nest at about three weeks of age. They still depend on Mom and Dad for another three weeks.

JUVENILE The young can date, mate and raise young at one year old.

Birding Tip

Make your own suet feeder. Suet is animal fat. In the wild, woodpeckers and chickadees eat the fat from a deer carcass. In town, you can buy beef suet at a grocery store. Place the suet in a mesh orange or onion bag, or pound it into the cracks of tree bark. With the help of an adult, melt suet over LOW heat. Place a string or yarn around the base of a pine cone and dip it into the melted suet. Add millet, peanut hearts and cornmeal. Hang your feeders outside on a tree limb.

When

Downy Woodpeckers are diurnal. They feed during the day and rest at night.

Migration

Permanent resident. Downy Woodpeckers remain in their breeding territory all year.

Nesting

Downy Woodpeckers begin pairing up as early as October or November in Michigan. Nesting begins in May and early June.

Getting Around

How do they stay on a tree while drilling a hole or searching for insects? Their toes are zygodactyl, which means two toes point forward and two backward. Their long, curved claws are super for getting a tight grip. Their stiff tail feathers act as a brace against the tree trunk. Look for a flash of white while the downy is in flight. The black barred tail has white outer feathers. Flight is undulating (up and down) in a series of wing flaps and then a bound forward.

Where to Look

Open deciduous woods of both old and new growth. Their ability to feed on many different foods allows Downy Woodpeckers to live in many places.
· All over Michigan

Year-round	Summer
Migration	Winter

Eastern Bluebird

Sialia sialis

Length: 7 inches
Wingspan: 13 inches

Short, stout bill slightly notched at the tip for catching insects

Male is sky blue above

Young look like females but are speckled, and have blue wings

Rusty-orange throat and breast

White belly

female

Females are duller in color than males

"Tury, cherwee, cheye-ley." Male loudly sings this song to claim his territory. The same song is sung softly to tell the female on the nest, "Everything's O.K., dear."

Wildlife Hotel: Immediate Occupancy

Bluebirds need tree cavities for nesting. Some people view an aging tree as useless and cut it down. An older tree or a rotting tree is a wildlife hotel complete with buffet dining, single occupancy or condominiums. In Michigan, folks teamed up and built bluebird nesting boxes and placed them along forest edges and open rural and suburban areas that bluebirds need for catching insects. Since then the number of Eastern Bluebirds in Michigan has increased. You can become a part of this success story by planting and leaving valuable habitat and building and monitoring your own bluebird nesting boxes. Learn more from the Michigan Bluebird Society, www.michiganbluebirdsociety.org

Habitat Café

Yumm ... bring an order of crickets, beetles, grasshoppers, ants, spiders, earthworms, snails and berries. Eastern Bluebirds are omnivorous. Put wiggly mealworms on the ground to invite a blue visitor. Most pet shops have mealworms.

SPRING, SUMMER, FALL MENU:
 Lots of insects, some fruits and berries

WINTER MENU:
 More fruits and berries than summer, but insects are still the main course

Life Cycle

NEST The female builds the nest cup of grasses in a natural tree cavity made by other birds such as woodpeckers, in the tops of rotten fence posts, or in nesting boxes.

EGGS About ½ inch long. The female incubates the clutch of 4–5 eggs for 12–14 days.

MOM! DAD! Altricial. The parents feed their young right after the chicks are born until three weeks after they leave the nest.

NESTLING The gray, downy chicks will begin to look like a female or male at about 1½ weeks of age. By then, their feathers have grown in and they leave the nest.

FLEDGLING If you hear *Tu-a-wee*, near a nesting cavity or box you will know that a young bluebird is leaving the nest to perch on a nearby limb or in cover. They also give this call when they are waiting for their parents to feed them.

JUVENILE In one year, they are mature enough to nest.

Unsolved Mystery

Is global warming affecting the seasonal movement of birds that nest in Michigan? Are they returning earlier, leaving later or not leaving at all? Solving this mystery requires clues (records) from people all over Michigan. In recent years individuals that have kept journals with bluebird departure and return dates have noted some significant changes. Keep your records in the journal section, pages 188–189. Be a part of solving this global mystery!

When

Eastern Bluebirds are diurnal. They feed during the day and rest at night.

Migration

Spring Arrival: March. Fall Departure: late Sept.–Nov. Short distance migrant as far as southeastern U.S. and northern Mexico. Some may stay all year.

Nesting

Eastern Bluebirds begin nesting in Michigan in April and May. They may raise 1–3 broods per summer.

Getting Around

Eastern Bluebirds sidle—they move sideways. They hop and walk sideways while turning halfway around. How does it scratch its head? By moving a foot up and over a drooping wing. They are true-blue acrobats! Bluebirds fly low in open areas, about 10–12 feet above the ground. Their flight is higher on longer journeys.

Where to Look

Open habitats along deciduous forest edges. More common in southern and western Michigan.
· Seven Ponds Nature Center
· Wint Nature Center
· Dahlem Nature Center

Year-round	Summer
Migration	Winter

Baltimore Oriole

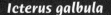

Icterus galbula

Length: 7–8 inches
Wingspan: 11–12 inches

Males are black with an orange breast, underside and wing shoulder

Young look like female

female

Females are brown-olive on back and faded yellow underneath. Wings have a white wing bar.

One white wing bar

Orange-and-black tail

"Tee-dee-dee."
Nestlings:
"Bring food, more food!"

Dealing with Imposters

The buffalo that once roamed the open prairies were not alone. Brown-headed Cowbirds followed them eating both insects they kicked up and insects living in their dung. Cowbirds didn't have time to sto and nest. Instead, they laid their eggs in the nests of birds that live where the prairie and forest mee A female cowbird lays up to 40 eggs each year, none of which she hatches. Baltimore Orioles are fore: edge nesters and recipients of cowbird eggs. Cowbirds do not reimburse the host species for incubatio meals and around the clock chick-care. Baltimore Orioles have adapted a strategy in turn. They push th cowbird eggs out of the nest. Their plan in dealing with imposter eggs generally works.

Habitat Café

Yumm . . . bring an order of caterpillars, grasshoppers, ants, beetles, spiders, blackberries, cherries, apples and raspberries. Fill a nectar feeder and watch orioles in your backyard. Baltimore Orioles are omnivorous and many birds can see UV or ultraviolet light. Many fruits reflect UV light but the leaves around them do not. This allows birds to zero in on their next snack!

SPRING, SUMMER, FALL, WINTER MENU:
 Mostly insects, some fruit

Life Cycle

NEST The female builds a pouch-like nest on the tip of a large tree branch. She hangs loops of plant fibers and long grass around the branch. Milkweed silk is woven through the loops to make a hanging basket 5–8 inches long. The pouch is lined with feathers and animal fur. Set out brightly colored string, yarn or fabric strips in your yard and she may weave them into her hanging work of art!

EGGS About 1 inch long. The female incubates the clutch of 4–5 eggs for 12–14 days.

MOM! DAD! Altricial. Mom and Dad make about 13 trips per hour to feed their hungry chicks.

NESTLING The chicks stay in the nest for about two weeks.

FLEDGLING When the young leave the nest, they can fly short distances. Mom and Dad bring the young birds food for two more weeks. They may take the kids to a nearby grape jelly feeder and stuff their beaks full of sticky jelly. Fresh green peas are popular, too.

JUVENILE In August, small flocks of juveniles group together and prepare for migration.

Did You Know

In their Costa Rica wintering grounds, orioles feed on the fruit and insects found in both the tropical lowland forests and on coffee plantations. Planting Inga trees between the rows shades the coffee trees and makes more habitat for wildlife. Migratory birds depend on habitat around the world for their survival. Well done, Costa Rica!

When

Baltimore Orioles are diurnal. They feed during the day and rest at night.

Migration

Spring Arrival: late April–May
Fall Departure: Mid-August–Sept
Long-distance migrant south along the Mississippi Flyway to Mexico and then to Central and South America.

Nesting

Baltimore Orioles begin nesting in May in Michigan.

Getting Around

Baltimore Orioles are strong fliers with powerful wing strokes. They hop from branch to branch to glean (pick up) insects. They can even hang upside down to eat fruit and weave their nests! This is a handy trick to know because it can take the female Baltimore Oriole nearly a week to finish weaving the sock-like nest. That's a long time to hang upside down!

Where to Look

Deciduous forest. Open woods and forest edges, parks, orchards and city neighborhoods where they visit backyard oriole feeders.
· Otis Audubon Sanctuary
· P.J. Hoffmaster State Park

Year-round	Summer
Migration	Winter

Northern Cardinal

Cardinalis cardinalis

Length: 8–9 inches
Wingspan: 12 inches

Red crest

Males are bright red

female

Females are gray-tan with
pale red on crest and wings

Red, conical bill
is shaped for
cracking open
hard seeds

Young look like female,
but with dark crest
and bill

"Chip, chip."
Male: "This is my territory."
"Took, took."
Female: "All clear. You
can bring the food to
the nest now."

Newcomer to Michigan

Northern Cardinals are fairly new to Michigan. They arrived in Michigan's southernmost counties during 1881–1920 from states to the south and east. What conditions brought these brilliant birds north? Northern Cardinals can live in different kinds of shrubby areas away from people or right in their backyards. They need just enough food, low shrubs and trees to nest in and raise their young. With the opening of forest edges and the creation of shrubby semi-open areas, and winter backyard bird feeders filled with safflower and sunflower seeds, cardinals are adding to their range in Michigan. Cardinals have moved to the north as far as the Upper Peninsula. Welcome!

Habitat Café

Yumm . . . bring an order of grasshoppers, cicadas, beetles, butterflies, moths, seeds and fruit. Cardinals are omnivorous. When the trees leaf out, they feed on leaf buds and insect larvae. In the fall, they eat seeds and fruit. Young chicks eat protein-rich insects.

SPRING, SUMMER, FALL MENU:
 Insects are the main course, with hearty helpings of seeds and fruits

WINTER MENU:
 Mainly seeds and fruits, some insects

Life Cycle

NEST The female builds the bowl-shaped nest in a thick tangle of shrubs or in a small tree within 10 feet of the ground. Using her bill, the female chews the twigs to make them easier to bend around her body. Then, sitting in the center of the nest and turning around, she pushes out with her feet against the twigs, grapevine bark, leaves or weed stems to form a cup. The nest is lined with fine grass.

EGGS About ⅜ inch long. The female incubates 2–3 eggs for 11–13 days. The male brings her food.

MOM! DAD! Altricial. Mom and Dad both care for the chicks.

NESTLING The gray downy chicks stay in the nest for 8–10 days while their feathers grow in.

FLEDGLING When young cardinals leave the nest at almost two weeks of age, they have small crests on their heads and can fly short distances. They perch on a nearby branch while Mom and Dad deliver food.

JUVENILE At one year of age most young have settled within five miles of where they were raised to sing their adult song, date, mate and raise their own young.

Unsolved Mystery

Why do some songbirds rub or hold ants on their feathers and skin? Why does a bird lay on an anthill and allow ants to crawl into its feathers? Biologists have not solved the mystery of this behavior, called anting. Ideas include: ants have an acid that protects birds against parasites, fungus and bacteria that could harm their feathers; it soothes their skin during feather molting; they store ants for eating later; and/or the ants' acid works to ready food for eating. Get antsy and solve the mystery!

When

Northern Cardinals are diurnal. They feed during the day and rest at night.

Migration

Permanent residents. To stay warm during Michigan's cold winters, a cardinal fluffs out its feathers to trap body heat and tucks its bill inside its wing.

Nesting

Northern Cardinals begin nesting in April in Michigan.

Getting Around

Northern Cardinals hop on the ground and take short flights from branch to branch when looking for insects and buds to eat. They clean and sharpen their bill by rubbing the edges of on something hard. On winter afternoons, they often become active before sunset, looking for a snack before they go to sleep.

Where to Look

Highest numbers are located in Michigan's southern LP, especially thick, shrubby areas of deciduous forests, farm windbreaks, urban woodlots and backyards.
- Sarett Nature Center
- Woldumar Nature Center

Year-round	Summer
Migration	Winter

Deciduous Forest Habitat

Rose-breasted Grosbeak

Pheucticus ludovicianus

Length: 7–8 1/2 inches
Wingspan: 12–13 inches

Large, white seed-eating bill

Black mask

female

Female streaked olive-brown and black above, with pale crown stripe, under parts with dark streaks on breast

Pink-red triangle on breast

While females look the same all year, males change to brown and white during the non-breeding season

White under-parts with faint streaks under wings

Song: Both male and female sing a song a bit like a robin, but sweeter. "See!"

Global Warming and Birds

Rose-breasted Grosbeaks, like other migratory birds, depend on habitat around the globe for survival. How does global warming affect birds? Is spring migration becoming earlier and fall migration later? Are nesting ranges moving north? Birds belong to a complex food web. Birds that nest in North America take advantage of the summer increase in insects (protein) to fuel their chicks' fast growth. This timing has evolved over thousands of years into a synchronized pattern of events. How does global warming affect the food web? Be a part of science and help find the answers. Join the National Audubon Society's "Great Backyard Bird Count" to record events in the natural world.

Habitat Café

Yumm . . . bring an order of tree buds, flowers, insects and fruit. Rose-breasted Grosbeaks are omnivorous, eating both plant and animal matter. They also help farmers by eating crop pests.

day's Special

sunflower, safflower, peanuts

SPRING, SUMMER MENU:
 Tree buds, insects and fruit

FALL MENU:
 Fruit

WINTER MENU:
 Insects and fruit

Life Cycle

NEST The loose cup nest is built by both the female and male in the fork of a deciduous tree commonly 7–12 feet above the ground. The loose and flimsy nest of twigs is lined with fine rootlets, grass, feathers or leaves.

EGGS About 1 inch long. Both parents incubate the clutch of 3–5 eggs for 11–14 days.

MOM! DAD! Altricial. Mom and Dad both feed the chicks, brood them and do their part in diaper duty. Parents make 50 or more feeding visits to the famished young per hour; now that's fast food.

NESTLING When danger is near, the nearly week old chicks do their "freeze" act to outsmart predators.

FLEDGLING With such fast growth, chicks leave the nest at 9–12 days of age. The egg tooth used to break out of the shell drops off in the second week. At this stage it would only add extra weight when trying to fly.

JUVENILE In one year, they are mature enough to nest and raise their own young.

Did You Know

On a moonlit September or April night when you lay quiet in your room, open the windows wide, pull your pillow to the windowsill and listen. The sky is alive. You may even hear the faint migration calls of some of the hundreds and thousands of birds passing overhead along the great migration skyway. Each species has a call they use during migration to communicate. It's a wonder that anyone can think of sleep on a night with wildlife on the move in the starry sky—the stuff of dreams!

When

Rose-breasted Grosbeaks are diurnal. They feed during the day and rest at night.

Migration

Spring Arrival late April–May Fall Departure late Aug–Oct Long-distance migrant to Central and South America. Migratory flight by night alone or in groups of 50 or more grosbeaks.

Nesting

Rose-breasted Grosbeaks begin nesting in May in Michigan.

Getting Around

Watch for the male's black-and-white wing marks during their strong up and down flight (fast then slow wing bursts). When on the ground or along a branch, they hop rather than walk.

Where to Look

Deciduous and mixed forests, edges, thickets, orchards, parks and gardens across most of Michigan.
- Mill Creek State Historic Park
- South Higgins Lake State Park

Year-round	Summer
Migration	Winter

American Robin

Turdus migratorius

Length: 9–11 inches
Wingspan: 15–16 inches

female

Gray above with very dark head, wings and tail

White eye-ring and white chin

Females not as brightly colored as males

"Red" breast—brown to dark red-orange

In flight, look for the white between their tummy and tail

Young have speckled breast and white flecks on their dark backs

White tips on outer tail feathers

Brown legs

"Cheerily, cheer-up, cheer-up, cheer-up, cheerily, cheer-up!" This cheery song is sung during the time of nesting and incubation.

Squirmy Worms & Super-sized Storage

When you spy our state bird, the American Robin, with its head turned to the side and looking with one eye at the ground, it is probably ready to pounce on an insect with its yellow bill. Rather than eat it right away, the robin may store the food in its stretchy esophagus to digest later. Robins eat about 14 feet of earthworms in one day. At this rate, how many feet of earthworms could a robin eat in a week? Do the math (answer on pages 194-195). In the winter, robins pack their esophagus full of berries before the sun goes down. They digest food from this storage space when their body needs a snack before morning. Delicious!

Habitat Café

Yumm . . . bring an order of earthworms, beetles, grasshoppers, larvae, crickets, spiders, berries and other fruits. American Robins are omnivorous. They need more protein rich-insects during egg-laying and molting season than in the winter.

day's Special

earthworms

SPRING, SUMMER, FALL MENU:

 Mostly fruit and berries, lots of insects

WINTER MENU:

 Mainly fruit and berries, some insects

Life Cycle

NEST The female builds the nest in the fork of a tree, on a fence post, a window ledge or a manmade nesting platform. The outside of the nest is made with dead grass and twigs. To get just the right shape, she uses the bend of her wing and presses from the inside. Next, she carries mud in her bill for the inside. She turns her body in the hollow of the cup for the final fitting. The nest is lined with soft, dead grass.

EGGS About 1 inch long. The female incubates the clutch of 3–4 bright blue eggs for 12–14 days.

MOM! DAD! Altricial. The chicks hatch without feathers. Their skin is so thin that you can see the inside of their tiny bodies.

NESTLING The chick that begs the soonest, stretches its neck the highest and holds it beak closest to the parent gets food first. During the first 10 days, each nestling gets 35–40 feedings per day.

FLEDGLING They leave the nest at about 2 weeks of age and stay on the ground, fed mostly by Dad while Mom prepares for the next brood. Leave fledglings for their parents to care for, and keep your cat inside.

JUVENILE In late August, juveniles form a flock and prepare to migrate south.

Birding Tip

Make a small mud puddle in your backyard. (It's a good idea to ask first.) Watch from afar as a female robin takes mud for building her nest. When you see a mud-covered female, you'll know her nest is nearby. Set out bright colored yarn and string. She may use this in her nest, too!

When

American Robins are diurnal. They feed during the day and rest at night.

Migration

Spring Arrival: March–April
Fall Departure: Late Sept.–Oct. Short distance migrant. Winters in southeastern states in areas without snow cover and plenty of food such as fruit from shrubs.

Nesting

American Robins begin nesting in April–May in Michigan. They raise one or two broods each year.

Getting Around

Robins are speedy, using their sturdy leg muscles to run and hop in the grass. You may see them stop and look around quickly for prey or predators, and then they are off and running again. During migration, robins are fast, straight fliers with their pointed wings (20–36 mph). They use their medium-length tail for steering through trees during a quick escape.

Where to Look

Most of Michigan in areas with open woods, forest edges, farm windbreaks, parks and backyards.
· Super Adaptor

| Year-round | Summer |
| Migration | Winter |

American Woodcock

Length: 11 inches
Wingspan: 18 inches

Long bill is extra sensitive to help find earthworms and soil insects

Short neck

Disguised in leaf brown and a feather pattern that looks like dead grass

Juveniles look like dully colored adults. They may have a dark gray band on their throat

Short legs

Male and female look alike

Whistling Wings: The sharp whistling comes from air rushing through the three narrow, stiff outer wing feathers.

Romance in the Skies

Romance in the skies requires low light. Go to an open field near a river, bog, or wet area in April–May when the faint light of dawn, dusk or moonlight casts only a whisper of your shadow—*shh*. Listen for the winged notes of the American Woodcock as he spirals to the moon and flutters to earth in an aerial dance. First, he shows his desire for a female as he struts on the short grass. Then, tail up and spread, he makes a peenting sound (buzz) every few seconds. Suddenly he rises, flying off at an angle in whistling circles ever higher until he reaches 200–300 feet. Like a falling star, he flickers through the sky, landing where he started and repeats his twilight ballad.

Habitat Café

Yumm ... bring an order of earthworms with a side of larvae, ants, slugs and snails. American Woodcocks are insectivores. They glean (pick up) insects with their long 2 ½-inch bill. Eyes are far back on head so they can see while their bill is in the ground.

SPRING, SUMMER, FALL MENU:
≈ Lots of earthworms, some insects and snails

WINTER MENU:
≈ More insects and snails than summer, but still mostly earthworms

Life Cycle

NEST The simple ground nest is a slight depression in the leaves. The female may line the rim of the nest with a few twigs.

EGGS About 1 ⅛ inches long. The female incubates the clutch of 4 eggs for 20–21 days. If the female is flushed from the nest during incubation, she may not return to it. Respect the needs of wildlife.

MOM! DAD! Precocial. The young chicks leave the nest as soon as they hatch. If in danger, they "freeze." Mom feeds the chicks for the first week. Then the young probe for earthworms and insects on their own. They begin to fly after about two weeks of age and are nearly full grown at four weeks.

JUVENILE Juvenile woodcocks set out on their own at 4–6 weeks of age to join with others on fields at night until fall migration. In Michigan, American Woodcock migration may be as early as August or as late as November.

Did You Know

A woodcock's bill is designed for pulling worms from the soil. The tips of the mandibles (jaws) can be moved apart while the base of the bill is held together (like a pair of pinchers or tweezers). Stick your pencil in the mud and pull it out. The hole will look like one made by a woodcock. Finding "pencil holes" as you explore Michigan's damp river forests is a clue that a woodcock may be near. You might also want to do some research about the woodcock's upside-down brain!

When
Crepuscular. They are active near sunrise and sunset when the light is dim. May feed in daylight.

Migration
Spring Arrival: March – April
Fall Departure: late Aug – Nov
Short-distance migrant. Migrate by night, low to the ground in small flocks to Tennessee, Arkansas, and the Gulf states.

Nesting
American Woodcocks nest in wooded areas near a wet area in Michigan in April - May.

Getting Around
American Woodcocks walk along the ground with their long bill ahead of them. Look for slender tracks in soft mud with 3 toes forward and 1 short toe backward. They can swim short distances and fly low to the ground in a zig-zag to avoid predators.

Where to Look
Areas with aspen and alder in the north and young maple and ash in the south. Also frequents shrubs near rivers or bogs. The highest population is in the northern half of Michigan's LP.
· Sleeping Bear Dunes NP
· Barry State Game Area

	Year-round	Summer
	Migration	Winter

Brown Thrasher

Toxostoma rufum

Length: 11–12 inches
Wingspan: 13 inches

juvenile

Immature thrashers look similar to the adults but with gray eyes and cream-colored spotting on the upper sides of their bodies

Yellow eye

Rusty colored upper body

Long, slightly curved bill used as a broom to sweep leaves aside and pick up insects

Rusty colored, long tail

White underside with streaks of dark brown

Males and females look alike

"Plant a seed, plant a seed, bury it . . ." The male's spring song declares his space and desire for a female.

Beethoven of the Forest

Beethoven, make room. The Brown Thrasher singing a catchy tune of double phrases is an expert composer. Thrashers are their own woodland orchestra, singing more than one note at a time and each note at a different intensity. Birds do not have vocal cords, like you do. A bird's voice box, or syrinx, has two independent chambers. Nerves from the left side of the syrinx stimulate the left chamber while nerves from the right side stimulate the right chamber. This allows the bird to duet with itself. Birds control volume by inflating air sacs that in turn put pressure on the muscles of the syrinx. Brown Thrashers can compose from over 1,000 different musical phrases resulting in more than 2,000 songs!

Habitat Café

Yumm . . . bring an order of grasshoppers, ants, beetles, acorns and berries. Brown Thrashers are omnivorous. They eat plant and animal matter, depending on the season.

day's Special

eanuts and
mealworms
IRD FEEDER TREAT

SPRING, SUMMER, FALL MENU:
 Mainly insects, lots of berries and fruit

WINTER MENU:
Fewer berries and more insects than spring, summer and fall

Life Cycle

NEST The female and male build the twig basket nest 2–5 feet above the ground in the fork of a tree or shrub. At times they will nest on the ground. The basket nest is made in four steps, beginning with a bulky base of twigs and vines woven together, followed by a layer of leaves, and then a layer of small roots, stems and twigs. Lastly, the nest is lined with small grass rootlets that they clean by stomping (thrashing) the dirt off with their feet. A very clean and cozy nest!

EGGS About 1 inch long. The female and male both incubate the clutch of 3–5 eggs for 11–12 days.

MOM! DAD! Altricial. Both parents feed and care for the quickly growing young. In just 9 days the chicks have their feathers.

NESTLING The downy chicks stay in the nest for 11–12 days.

FLEDGLING Parents stay with the young for the first month. Gradually, the parents bring less and less food as the young become more independent.

JUVENILE They are ready to date, mate and raise their own young when spring comes around.

Did You Know

Listen for the repeating phrases for a sure clue that you are tapping in time to the Beethoven of the forest. "Plant-a-seed, plant-a-seed, bury-it, bury-it, cover-it-up, cover-it-up, let-it-grow, let-it-grow, pull-it-up, pull-it-up, eat-it, eat-it, yum-yum, yum-yum." Do Brown Thrashers sing these words? No, people give words to bird sounds to help them remember and identify them. Trek to the woods to listen to their song firsthand and compose your own phrases. Be creative!

When

Brown Thrashers are diurnal, active during the day and resting at night.

Migration

Spring Arrival: April–May
Fall Departure: Sept–Oct
They are short-distance migrants moving to the southern United States in the winter, preferring areas that stay above freezing (+32 degrees F). Some may remain in southern Michigan during mild winters, where they feed on berries and tree fruits.

Nesting

In Michigan, Brown Thrashers build their nest in May and lay their eggs in May and June.

Getting Around

Brown Thrashers spend most of their time on the ground walking and running after insects and hopping over brush and small trees. Their flight is low to the ground from shrub to shrub. Long, heavy legs are built to kick up leaves from the forest floor.

Where to Look

Shrubby, deciduous forest edges, wooded fence rows, farm wind-breaks and wooded parks with open areas. Especially in the Lower Peninsula.

Year-round	Summer
Migration	Winter

Deciduous Forest Habitat

93

Mourning Dove

Zenaida macroura

Length: 11–13 inches
Wingspan: 18 inches

side profile

Dark brown eyes with an edge of blue skin; one black spot below.

Small head with a bluish crown

Males have a rosy colored breast

Light gray above and buff below with black spot on wing and tail

Females have a tan breast and brown crown and are smaller than males

Short, red legs and fleshy red feet

Young are mottled with white wing tips

"Coo-oo, OO-OO-OO." The male's call to attract a female. Try this. Blow softly across the neck of an open bottle. It will sound similar to a dove.

Long tail that comes to a point

Cooing All Over Michigan

Coo-oooo-oo-oo… You may wake up to the soothing coos of a love-struck Mourning Dove in Ann Arbor, Big Rapids or Kalamazoo. You may hear the whistle of their wings on a farm near Albion or farther north near Indian River. Word has it that they have even been heard around Cheboygan and Escanaba. Mourning Doves are Super Adaptors, able to live in many different habitats all over Michigan. As long as they can find seeds to eat and cover to nest in, Mourning Doves will be in our cities, farms, parks and suburban neighborhoods. Spread cracked corn on the ground. A cooing neighbor may come close enough to sketch, photograph or to simply enjoy their coo….mpany.

Habitat Café

Yumm . . . bring an order of seeds. Mourning Doves are herbivores. They eat seeds scattered over short grass and from bird feeders with a perch. At times, they will eat insects. Fill your backyard bird bath, birds need water every day!

SPRING, SUMMER, FALL, WINTER MENU:

 Almost all seeds

day's Special

millet and nflower seeds

BIRD FEEDER TREAT

Life Cycle

NEST The nest is built in a tree or shrub, in an old nest of another bird such as a robin, on the ledge of a building or on the ground. Both parents make the flimsy platform nest of twigs and line it with finer twigs.

EGGS About ⅞ inch long. For over two weeks, Dad incubates the 2 eggs during the day and Mom takes the night shift.

MOM! DAD! Altricial. For the first week, Mom and Dad feed the young crop milk. This bird baby formula is a secretion from their crop that has water, minerals high in vitamin A and B, and a higher protein and fat content than human or cow's milk! Seeds are gradually added at an increasing rate each day.

NESTLING At least one parent stays at the nest at all times.

FLEDGLING Young leave the nest at about two weeks of age. They continue to be fed some seeds by Dad in decreasing amounts until they are about one month of age when they forage for seeds on their own. Mom is busy getting ready for another brood.

JUVENILE Juveniles flock with other immature doves and move to areas with plentiful food, such as fields of harvested wheat.

Did You Know

Mourning Doves pick up as many seeds from the ground as their bi-lobed crop will hold. The seeds are digested later in the safety of their nesting and roosting site. A bird's crop is a large sac at the bottom of the esophagus. How many seeds can a Mourning Dove's crop hold? The highest number recorded was over 17,000 bluegrass seeds!

When

Mourning Doves are diurnal. They feed during the day and rest at night.

Migration

Spring Arrival: March–April
Fall Departure: August–October
Short to long distance migrant to central and southern regions of the U.S. Some travel as far as Mexico and Costa Rica while some Mourning Doves may overwinter in southern Michigan.

Nesting

Mourning Doves begin nesting in Michigan in March-April and may continue through August. Raises 1–4 broods per year.

Getting Around

Mourning Doves walk or run on the ground when foraging for food rather than hopping. They move south in the cold months because their fleshy feet are easily frostbitten. In flight, Mourning Doves are swift, changing direction and height quickly.

Where to Look

All of Michigan, except the deep, thick coniferous and deciduous forests. Look for Mourning Doves in your neighborhood!
· Super Adaptor

| Year-round | Summer |
| Migration | Winter |

Northern Flicker

Colaptes auratus

Length: 12–13 inches
Wingspan: 20 inches

Gray-brown with dark bars above

Red patch on gray crown

Long bill

Male has black mustache

Black bib on upper breast

Bright yellow under wings and tail and shaft of flight feathers

White rump patch shows in flights

Male defends space with a loud, "wika-wika-wika" and flicks open wings and tail to show his bright underside.

Anteater-on-Wings

What eats the most ants of any North American bird? What member of the woodpecker family rarely pecks? The Northern Flicker. Rather than peck wood out of a tree for a nest hole, Northern Flickers choose a rotten tree and dig out the punky (soft) wood. They generally don't use their bill to peck for food either. Anteaters-on-wings, flickers probe the forest soil with their bill and snap ants up with their 3-inch long, sticky tongue. Invite flickers by keeping dead trees as wildlife hotels. Build and place nest boxes filled with sawdust too. Once flickers come and nest, you may have long-time lodgers. They often return to the same site each year!

Habitat Café

Yumm . . . bring an order of ants and beetles with side orders of grasshoppers, topped with wild fruits and berries, a few seeds and nuts. Northern Flickers are omnivorous, eating both plant and animal matter. A researcher counted some 5,000 ants in just one flicker!

SPRING & SUMMER MENU:
 Mostly insects with some fruits and berries

FALL, WINTER MENU:
 Berries of trees, shrubs and vines with some insects

Life Cycle

NEST Both the male and female chisel away wood in a dead or dying tree, called a snag. Flickers also use fence posts, poles and nest boxes packed with sawdust. The nest tree is generally located near anthills.

EGGS About 1 inch long. The clutch of 5-8 eggs is incubated by both parents for about 11-14 days.

MOM! DAD! Altricial. Parents store ant larvae in their crop and deliver this lunch to their young by spitting it back up.

NESTLING A peck in the chick's heel or rump is a signal from Mom and Dad that it is diaper duty time. Parents eat the sacs for the first ten days and carry the sacs away from the nest from then on.

FLEDGLING The young leave the nest when they are nearly four weeks of age and generally in the order that they hatched.

JUVENILE Watch for flicker families filling up on ants near anthills in late summer. At one year old, flickers are able to drum-and-date, mate and raise their own family.

Did You Know

An important part of the forest ecosystem, flicker nests are recycled by American Kestrels and some ducks. European Starlings are a different matter. They will barge in an active flicker nest, take out the eggs and set up house. Red squirrels will kill young flickers in the nest. Buzzzzzz . . . beware. When threatened, young flickers mimic the sound of a swarm of bees. So long, predators!

When

Diurnal. Flickers are active during the day and rest at night.

Migration
Spring Arrival: March–April
Fall Departure: Sept–Oct.
Short distance migrant flying mostly by night to areas in the southern U.S. Some flickers over-winter in the southern half of Michigan's LP.

Nesting
Flickers begin egg-laying May–June in Michigan in areas with dead and dying trees or in nest boxes.

Getting Around
Flickers hop when on the ground, on a tree or limb. Like most members of the woodpecker family, their flight is up-and-down, called undulating. The stiff tail is used as a prop when drumming on a tree or chiseling a nest hole.

Where to Look
Forest edges and open woodlands bordering fields.
· Seney National Wildlife Area
· Hiawatha National Forest
· Hartwick Pines State Park

Year-round	Summer
Migration	Winter

Deciduous Forest Habitat

Eastern Screech-Owl

Megascops asio

Length: 8–10 inches
Wingspan: 20–22 inches

Ear tufts mimic sticks

Two color-morphs: gray and rufous (rust)

Yellow eyes and bill

Male and female look alike, females generally larger

Large feet and feathered toes

Begins calling in February and March in Michigan. Makes a trill, bark, hoot, rasp, chuckle and "Screech!"

Magicians Among Us

Magicians live in the trees of Michigan. One may even live near your yard, school or local park. You will need to learn their magic tricks to find them. Under the veil of darkness they perch on a limb to stalk their next meal. When the light of day materializes, they hide in the chamber of a tree or hollow limb, perhaps staring right at you. Their secret to being invisible? They sit straight up to look like tree bark, raise their ears tufts like tree sticks, squint their eyes to mere slits and hold their feathers and wings tight against their body. If you are very close, they may shift sideways and raise a wing like cloak of invisibility, covering all but their eyes. Abracadabra!

Habitat Café

Yumm . . . bring an order of songbirds, squirrels, bats, moles, mice, rabbits, snakes, toads, frogs, crayfish, salamanders, beetles, moth larvae, crickets, grasshoppers, cicadas and fish. Eastern Screech-Owls are carnivorous. Active at night, they capture prey with their feet.

SPRING & SUMMER MENU:
 More insects and birds

FALL & WINTER MENU:
 More small mammals

Life Cycle

NEST Why go to all the effort to build or bring in nesting materials when an old squirrel or bird nest can be recycled? True conservationists, screech-owls lay their eggs right on the old nests in tree and limb hollows, or a stump. It is generally 13–20 feet from the ground. The nest floor may have old leaves, rotted wood, or leftovers from previous renters.

EGGS About 1 ½ inch long. The female incubates the clutch of 3–5 eggs for 26-30 days. The male may bring her food.

MOM! DAD! Altricial. The chicks depend on Dad to bring food and Mom to tear it into bite-size pieces.

NESTLING Chicks cooperate in keeping the nest corners for defecation. They practice their first vocals, making eerie trills, hoots and screeches into the night darkness.

FLEDGLING At about four weeks the chicks leave the nest for a nearby limb or tree. Mom and Dad deliver meals for 8–10 weeks while the young practice being predators, pouncing on objects and learning to cache food.

JUVENILE At one year of age, they can nest and raise their own woodland magicians. Poof!

Did You Know

You can make a simple nest box for screech-owls. Use lumber about ¾" inch thick; 2 ¾" inch diameter entrance hole, its bottom 10 inches above floor; front-sloping lid 2 inches above entrance hole, overhanging 1 inch, hinged at back, hooked at side; floor 7 x 7 inches with nail-sized drain holes in bottom corners. Place the box 10-13 ft. high on a tree trunk in a shady area about 100 feet from any other owl nest box or cavity. Sprinkle about one inch of dry leaf litter on the bottom. Have fun!

When 🌙
Nocturnal. Eastern Screech-Owls are active at night (nocturnal) and sometimes at dawn and dusk, called crepuscular.

Migration
Permanent resident. Eastern Screech-Owls stay in Michigan all year.

Nesting
Eastern Screech-Owls usually lay their eggs in April–May in Michigan in nest boxes, the hollow of a tree, or in recycled tree cavities dug out by flickers and woodpeckers.

Getting Around
Screech-owls fly low through the forest in a steady flight. To disguise where they land, they make a sudden U-turn up to a new perch. To capture prey on the ground, they walk, hop or run.

Where to Look
Brushy edges and borders of deciduous forests in Michigan's LP, especially the southern half. Mature deciduous trees with nesting cavities in places like city parks, backyards, schoolyards, rural woodlots and along rivers and lakes.
· Lake Bluff Audubon Sanctuary

Year-round	Summer
Migration	Winter

Deciduous Forest Habitat   99

Cooper's Hawk

Accipiter cooperii

Length: 15–19 inches
Wingspan: 27–37 inches

soaring

juvenile

Red eyes

Gray above; underside is white with rust-colored bars

Short, rounded wings for cruising around trees

Immature: Yellow eyes. Brown back with brown bars below.

Females are ⅓ larger than the males

Long gray tail with black bands and a white tip

"Cak-cak-cak!" This call is given by males and females when the nest is in danger or the bird is excited.

Small Birds Beware—Accipiter in the Area!

The eyes have it. Cooper's Hawks have eyes so large there is little room left in their skull to move them. Hawks move their entire head from side to side, and up and down to get a full range of vision. They are equipped with a monocle, a pair of binoculars and a telescope! Monocular vision allows each eye to see a separate image. The bird can scan and search for prey. Once located, binocular vision (both eyes seeing forward) allows the bird to judge the distance and depth of moving prey. Telescopic vision then allows the hawk to zero in on prey by making the image larger. Small birds beware—a Cooper's Hawk with eyes nearly as large as its stomach may be spying on you!

Habitat Café

Yumm . . . bring an order of Mourning Doves, robins, Blue Jays, starlings, chipmunks, rabbits, squirrels and mice with a side of frog. Cooper's Hawks are carnivorous. During nesting season, prey may be cached in a roost tree.

SPRING, SUMMER, FALL, WINTER MENU:

 Mainly birds, with a few mammals, reptiles, amphibians and insects

day's Special

bats

Life Cycle

NEST The male and female build the bulky twig and stick nest 20–60 feet high in a deciduous or coniferous tree. The 2-foot-wide nest is lined with small chips or flakes of bark.

EGGS About 1½ inches long. The female incubates the clutch of 4–5 eggs for 24–36 days.

MOM! DAD! Altricial. Mom broods the young for the first two weeks. She spreads her wings as a rain or sun umbrella.

NESTLING Dad brings the food and Mom tears the prey into bite-sized pieces. Parents carry away food pellets and uneaten food. Diaper duty? Not in this nest. The young are able to scoot to the rim of the nest and take care of this stinky job on their own.

FLEDGLING The young leave the nest when they are about one month old. Mom and Dad continue to bring food for nearly two more months.

JUVENILE At two years of age they are ready to date, mate and raise their own young.

Do the Math

$\begin{array}{r} 2 \\ +1 \\ \hline \end{array}$

In a study of a Cooper's Hawk nest, researchers found that it took an average of 66 robin-sized prey to raise one young hawk to the age of six weeks. How many prey would parent hawks need to capture for a family of three chicks over six weeks? Four chicks? Five chicks? Where do they find prey? Watch your bird feeders. Cooper's Hawks will come to bird feeders. Answer on pages 194-195.

When

Cooper's Hawks are diurnal. They feed during the day and rest at night.

Migration

Spring Arrival: April–May
Fall Departure: Sept–Oct
Short- to long-distant migrant to the southern United States, Mexico and Central America. Some overwinter in southern half of LP Michigan.

Nesting

Cooper's Hawks begin nesting in late March–April.

Getting Around

Cooper's Hawks fly low to the ground in a series of fast wing beats and then a swift glide. Gliding saves energy, and uses $\frac{1}{20}$ the energy of normal flight.

Where to Look

Deciduous and mixed deciduous-coniferous forests, often near a river or lake. They hunt along forested edges.
· Thompson's Harbor SP
· Lake Erie Metropark - migration
· Whitehouse Nature Center
· Timberland Swamp Nature Sanctuary

Year-round	Summer
Migration	Winter

Deciduous Forest Habitat

Pileated Woodpecker

Dryocopus pileatus

Length: 16–19 inches
Wingspan: 29 inches

feeding young

female

Female has a red crest.
She does not have a red
mustache or forehead.

Zebra-striped cheeks;
males have a red mustache
under their bill

The male raises
his red crest to
look bigger when
defending his area,
or to look "cool"
for a female

Strong feet have
two toes facing
forward and two
facing backward
for grasping and
balancing

"DRUM, DRUM
drum, drum."
Male: "This is my territory,
males stay away.
Females welcome!"

There's No Place Like Home

To a pair of Pileated Woodpeckers, there's no place like their home territory, all 150–200 acres. In Michigan, these old growth, thick, forested areas are found along rivers and lakes. Pileated Woodpeckers chisel 1–16 holes in a large, soft tree. The tree must be at least 16 inches in diameter. Do they use all the holes? Rarely. Extra holes are used by forest mammals, reptiles and amphibians for safe, warm places to sleep and nest. Bird buddies include House Wrens and Downy, Hairy and Red-bellied Woodpeckers. In coniferous forests, Red-breasted Nuthatches and Northern Saw-whet Owls owe a chirp of thanks to the largest woodpecker in the neighborhood.

Habitat Café

Yumm . . . bring an order of carpenter ants and wood-boring beetles and larvae with a side order of wild berries, nuts and suet. Pileated Woodpeckers are omnivorous. They use their very sticky, forked tongue to spear insects. Look for tree holes up to two feet long for a clue that this large woodpecker has been in the area for lunch.

SPRING, SUMMER, FALL, WINTER MENU:
 Lots of insects, some seeds

Life Cycle

NEST Each year the male and female bore a new nesting hole 15–70 feet above the ground in a soft, deciduous or coniferous tree. The entrance hole is 3¼ inches wide by 3½ inches long and 1–2 feet deep.

EGGS About 1¼ inches long. Both the female and male incubate the clutch of 3–4 eggs for 15–18 days. Dad incubates at night and Mom during the day.

MOM! DAD! Altricial. Chicks hatch naked, unable to see and with the remains of the yolk sac still attached to their belly. Both parents bring regurgitated insects until the chicks can digest them whole.

NESTLING Feathers begin at 10–16 days of age. At 15 days, the young peek out of the entrance hole with a "chrr—chrr" call when they see their parents.

FLEDGLING At three weeks of age, the young leave the nest, flying nearly 100 yards without any warm-up or practice!

JUVENILE For the next several months, the young are fed a few meals by their parents. They leave in the fall and find their own territory to date, mate, nest and raise their own young in the spring.

Do the Math

How many drumbeats can a woodpecker drum? If they make 15 drumbeats in one second, how many drumbeats can a woodpecker drum in one minute? Ten minutes? __ (your answer here.) How do woodpeckers drum without getting a big headache? Shock absorbers. Strong neck muscles and an extra-thick skull help cushion the brain. Answers on pages 196-197.

When

Pileated Woodpeckers are diurnal, active during the day and resting at night.

Migration

Permanent resident. Pileated Woodpeckers remain in their breeding territory all year.

Nesting

Michigan's largest woodpecker needs 150–200 acres of mature forest for nesting and breeding territory per pair. Egg laying and incubation begin in late April–May in Michigan. Listen for courtship drumming – they will even use telephone poles!

Getting Around

Watch for their white wing patches that flash in a slow but high-energy flight of gliding and quick wing-strokes. Pileated Woodpeckers climb up trunks with the use of their strong feet and stiff, supportive tail.

Where to Look

Michigan's deciduous and mixed coniferous-deciduous old-growth forests and areas along rivers and lakes and swamps. Most common in Michigan's U.P. and the northern half and west of the L.P.
- Haymarsh Lake State Game Area
- Chippewa National Forest

Year-round	Summer
Migration	Winter

Deciduous Forest Habitat   103

Barred Owl

Strix varia

Length: 17–24 inches
Wingspan: 42 inches

landing

Yellow beak

Dark blue eyes
surrounded by
facial disc that
looks like huge
glasses

Gray-brown
with bars across
its breast

Brown downward
streaks on the
pale belly

Females and males
look alike with females
generally larger.

Young look like
the adults

"Who cooks for you, who
cooks for you all?"
Most common in
February—early March
in Michigan.

Of Friend and Foe

Barred Owls and Red-shouldered Hawks hang out in the same habitat. They have an understanding. This is not the case between Barred Owls and Great Horned Owls. In small forest spaces and broken-up forests, Barred Owls move out when Great Horned Owls move in. Why? Great Horned Owls kill Barred Owls. They kill the young Barred Owls in the nest, young that have just left the nest, and even adults. In larger forested areas, all is well. Each species has enough space to spread out and establish territories and there is a greater supply of food. Friend or foe? Habitat is the key.

Habitat Café

Yumm . . . bring an order of small mammals, a few small birds, and a couple reptiles and amphibians. Barred Owls are carnivorous. They will hang around bird feeders to catch the mice and voles that are attracted to fallen seed on the ground.

SPRING, SUMMER, FALL, WINTER MENU:

 Mostly mammals, some birds, reptiles, amphibians and insects

Life Cycle

NEST Barred Owls use a hollow tree cavity or an old hawk, crow, heron or squirrel nest in the top of a tall tree. The recycled nest may be lined with some of their own feathers. They will also use a nesting box.

EGGS About 1½ inches long. The female incubates the clutch of 2–3 eggs for 28–33 days.

MOM! DAD! Altricial. As soon as they hatch, the white fuzz balls call and beg for food. Dad hunts and Mom tears the food into soft bite-sized pieces. She stays at the nest for most of the first two weeks, warming the chicks until their larger feathers grow in.

NESTLING Starting after the third week, Dad leaves prey in the nest while Mom is gone. They learn to tear apart their own dinner.

FLEDGLING The young leave the nest still unable to fly when they are 4–5 weeks old and perch on a branch as they wait for Mom and Dad to bring food. Flying lessons begin when they are 10 weeks of age.

JUVENILE Mom and Dad bring food until early fall, when the teens move away to establish their own spaces. They are mature enough to date, mate and raise their own young when they are 2 years old.

Did You Know

Our ears do not hear the full range of sounds that birds make. How do we know? We can see the bird sounds that we hear and don't hear on an electric sonogram. When you hear an echo in the forest darkness that sounds like monsters going mad, this may be a pair of Barred Owls "jiving," a duet of hoots, caws, cackles and gurgles. All this ruckus to impress and bond to each other. Of course, they sleep during the day!

When

Nocturnal, active during the night and resting during the day. Hunting is done mostly right after dark and just before dawn.

Migration

Permanent resident: Barred Owls live all year in Michigan.

Nesting

Barred Owls get an early wing up on the nesting season. They begin to nest and lay eggs in early March–early May in Michigan.

Getting Around

Barred Owls perch in trees to listen and watch for movement of prey below. Once alerted to prey, the owl drops like a bullet on silent wings to snatch its target. They have paths they use routinely through their territory.

Where to Look

Mature (older) deciduous and mixed deciduous-coniferous forests in Michigan except the southeast corner of the LP.

· Binder Park Zoo and
  Wildlife Area
· Chippewa National Forest
· Hiawatha National Forest
· Grass River Natural Area

Year-round   Summer
Migration   Winter

Deciduous Forest Habitat   105

Great Horned Owl

Bubo virginianus

Length: 18–25 inches
Wingspan: 3–5 feet

Ear tufts. Only large Michigan owl with long, feathered ear tufts.

Very large, yellow eyes

in flight

Hooked beak to tear the muscles and bones of prey

Facial disc of feathers funnel sound waves to their ears for extraordinary hearing

spitting pellet

Both males and females have brown, black and cream lines over most of their body with a white bib

Females are heavier and larger than males

"Who-hoo-ho-oo?" or, "This is my territory." Hooting duets between paired males and females can be heard from January until the first eggs are laid.

Flying Mousetrap

The hooting of Great Horned Owls can wake you up just about anywhere in Michigan, whether you are tucked under your winter covers or wrapped in summer's heat with fireflies lighting your room. Winter is the best time to listen for owls, but I've been driven to giggles on summer nights listening to young owls practicing their whooing. *Super Adaptors*, they live in cities, rural farming areas and places in between. They need a large tree for nesting and plenty of mice, rabbits, squirrels and skunks for the taking. The full menu includes stray cats and animals as large as porcupines! Hear a Great Horned Owl in the night and know that this flying mousetrap is hard at work in your neighborhood.

Habitat Café

Yumm . . . bring an order of mice, rabbits, hares, ground squirrels, muskrats, squirrels, pocket gophers, snakes, small birds, pheasants, ducks and geese. They may take animals as large as raccoons, skunks, porcupines or Great Blue Herons. Great Horned Owls are carnivorous.

SPRING, SUMMER, FALL, WINTER MENU:
 Mostly mammals, a few birds

Life Cycle

NEST These big owls do not make their own nest. They use a hollow tree cavity or an old hawk, crow, heron or squirrel nest in the top of a tall tree. Owls may line the recycled nest with some of their own feathers.

EGGS About 2 inches long. The female incubates the clutch of 2–3 eggs for 28–33 days. She does not leave the eggs for more than a few minutes at a time to keep them from freezing.

MOM! DAD! Altricial. Cold, wind and snow means the Mom broods the young downy chicks for the first three weeks. Dad brings food. As feathers replace the down, Mom leaves to hunt too.

NESTLING Able to feed themselves at about four weeks of age.

FLEDGLING At six weeks of age, young owls venture out to nearby branches. Their first test flights begin the following week.

JUVENILE Teenage owls stay with their parents during the summer and set out to find their own territories in late fall and early winter. At two years of age, they are able to mate and raise their own young.

Gross Factor

What does an owl do with the bones and fur of their eaten prey? Form them into a pellet and spit them back up. You'll know you're under an owl roost when you find gray, 2–3 inch pellets. Break open a compact pellet and you may discover the tiny bones of a mouse, the jawbone of a rabbit, spine sections of a gopher and the beak of a starling, all surrounded by undigested fur. WOW!

When
Nocturnal. Feeds at night and rests during the day. At times, they will hunt during the day.

Migration
Permanent resident. Stays all year in Michigan. Many predators fly south for the winter, leaving Great Horned Owls to take advantage of less competition for prey.

Nesting
Michigan's earliest nesting bird, it nests in late January and early February in the L.P. This adaptation may provide them with enough time for the young to mature and lets them take advantage of greater food availability.

Getting Around
Silent flight. An extra fuzzy covering over the flight feathers quiets the rush of air over the short, wide, powerful wings. It tucks its head in and holds its wings straight out, alternating strong wing beats with glides. On the ground, it walks in alternating steps.

Where to Look
Statewide, but more common in southern LP. Look for it in open areas, perched on poles, fence posts, trees and rock outcrops scanning for food.
· *Super Adaptor*

Year-round	Summer
Migration	Winter

Wild Turkey

Meleagris gallopavo

Length: 3–4 feet
Wingspan: 4–5½ feet

non-displaying male

female

Hens wear dull brown camouflage

Broad, rounded wings and tail. Toms (males) have a tail that spreads into a large fan.

Bare red and blue head and neck with wattle (bumpy skin under the chin that puffs out)

Male: Long, black beard; modified feather tufts 9 inches or more

Body or contour feathers are broad and squared on the ends

"Gobble, gobble!" or, "This is my territory! Males stay away. Females come over!"

Long legs, with spur on back—both males and females have spurs, but only the young males' grow into pointed and curved spurs up to 2 inches long

Gobblers Galore

Habitat loss. Hunting without limits. Wild Turkeys lost their place in the deciduous woods of the upper Midwest from the 1800s to early 1900s. The final record of a Wild Turkey in Michigan was in 1897. Teamwork between the Michigan DNR, the Michigan Wild Turkey Hunters Association and the National Turkey Federation brought Wild Turkeys back to a sustainable level (enough turkeys to survive over time) in Michigan. These efforts included bringing Wild Turkeys from Missouri and Iowa to repopulate Michigan's deciduous woods. The relocated turkeys produced little jakes and jennies galore. Today more than 200,000 Wild Turkeys roam Michigan. Happy Thanksgiving!

Habitat Café

Yumm . . . bring an order of buds, ferns, bugs, seeds, fruit, grass, nuts (acorns), field grains and more. Wild Turkeys are omnivorous.

SPRING, SUMMER, FALL MENU:
Fruit, berries, insects and plants

FALL MENU:
Acorns and hickory nuts

WINTER MENU:
Corn and other grains from fields

day's Special
bbles that go
o the gizzard
grind food

Life Cycle

NEST The female builds the nest in dead leaves on the ground, often hidden under a log, in a bush or at the base of a tree. She lines the nest depression with dry leaves. Mom camouflages the nest and eggs with more leaves when she takes a recess from incubation.

EGGS About 2½ inches long. The female incubates the clutch of 8–15 eggs for 27–28 days. Dad is busy grouping up with his harem of several females.

MOM! DAD! Precocial and downy. The newly hatched chicks leave the nest within one day of hatching. Mom leads them to food where they feed on protein-rich insects, seeds and berries. For warmth and protection from predators, the chicks nestle under Mom's wing next to her body. The young birds have their wing feathers and can fly at two weeks of age. They fly up to a nearby tree branch where they spend the night roosting.

JUVENILE The brood stays together until winter when several hens and their broods join together in a large flock. Toms and jakes form their own flocks.

Gross Factor

How do you know if you are on the trail of a tom or hen? Scat. Poop. Yes, male and female turkeys leave different scat. Males, or toms, leave a J-shaped scat over ⅜-inch in diameter. Females, or hens, leave a curly clump less than ⅜ inch in diameter. Look also for the tracks of wild turkeys that are typically 4–5 inches long and 4¼–5¼ inches wide. Turkeys use their feet to uncover insects, acorns and field corn. Look for scratch marks in the snow, too.

When

Wild Turkeys are diurnal, active during the day, feeding in the early morning and afternoon, and resting in trees at night.

Migration

Permanent resident. Wild Turkeys stay in Michigan all year.

Nesting

Wild Turkey males begin gobbling in early March and nesting begins in April in Michigan.

Getting Around

Flies straight up then away, hard and fast through the treetops at speeds of up to 55 mph over short distances. Can run 18 mph for short distances.

Where to Look

Forested areas near open farm fields, wooded areas near rivers, and brushy grasslands mainly in central and southern Michigan.
- Lost Nation Trail
- Yankee Springs Recreation Area
- Negwegon State Park
- Grass River Natural Area

Year-round   Summer
Migration   Winter

Prairie and Open Grasslands

Think like an Eastern Meadowlark. It needs water, insects for food, tall plants for perches, and a lot of open space without trees. The prairies and open grasslands of Michigan are just what a meadowlark needs.

Key to the Future

A prairie is land covered with native grasses and flowering plants with few to no trees at all. Why? Over ten thousand years ago, the Wisconsin Glacier (a mile-high slab of ice) stretched into Michigan. As

Fragmented prairie.

it grew southward it scraped the land, taking with it rocks and soil. When the glacier thawed, the meltwater formed potholes (wetlands) and lakes. The glacier also left behind rocks and dirt, called glacial till. This laid the base for plants to grow.

As the tallgrass prairie plants died back each year and decayed, new soil formed. This cycle went on for thousands of years, creating soil full of nutrients and home to an incredible variety of wild plants and animals.

When European settlement began in the early-mid 1800s in Michigan, the state hosted over 80,000 acres of prairie. Tallgrass prairies and oak savannas were scattered across the southern Lower Peninsula, while dry sand and wet prairies extended further north. Today less than one percent of Michigan's original native prairies remain, and these are mostly in small remnants, restored and reconstructed prairies. Efforts to save what is left and to recreate prairies offer keys to your future. Go to a prairie. Find the treasures and solve the mysteries that are waiting for you!

Land use changes over the past 170 years have altered the Michigan landscape dramatically. The scattered prairies and vast forests that once stretched across the state have been replaced by agricultural fields. The associated roadsides, pastures, hayfields and grasslands offer habitat to birds adapted to living in open areas. Ring-necked Pheasants take advantage of leftover field corn for food energy and the shelter of cornstalks for group huddles during winter storms.

Mind-boggling Plants

When you visit a native prairie you'll find plants that adapted to survive harsh conditions. Summer is hot and windy with occasional droughts (long periods without water). Winter brings cold, snow and more wind.

Canada anemone

Many prairie plants send their roots deep to reach water, anchoring themselves against the strong prairie winds. The Compass Plant grows a taproot ten feet into the soil. Other plants send out many fine roots just a few inches under the soil. And if it's cold? Put on a fur coat! The Pasque Flower does: it grows extra hairs that act like fur and protect it from extreme temperatures.

Dry prairie areas have shorter plants and wet areas host taller plants. In fact, a hundred or more years ago a man could be seen bumping across wet prairies riding an invisible horse. The horse was hidden by tall, six- to seven-foot grass! Plants that bloom early have short stalks. Plants that bloom later in the summer send up tall stalks to reach the sunlight. The Canada Anemone even grows sections like floors to a high-rise building, adding a "floor" as the prairie grows taller over the summer. In a native prairie there can be more than 25 different kinds of plants in just one square foot. Each species of plant plays host to prairie wildlife.

Incredible Critters

Insects, amphibians, reptiles, mammals and birds have adapted too. American Goldfinches don't migrate south with other birds. They put on a coat of extra feathers and stay for the winter, feeding in large flocks. American Kestrels scan the roadsides until snow covers the ground and then head farther south to find prey. Horned Larks return to Michigan as early as February, getting a jump on the nesting season.

American Goldfinch in winter plumage

Public areas and areas managed by groups like The Nature Conservancy and the Michigan Nature Association are great places to spy on birds and view native prairies. You can also find prairie birds in open grasslands, roadsides and field edges across much of the state. Prairie wildlife is calling for you!

When you spot prairie birds, use these pages to check them off this list. The locations of these illustrations indicate where you might see them.

American Goldfinch

Carduelis tristis

Length: 5 inches
Wingspan: 9 inches

male winter

female

Females are olive-green with pale yellow chest and throat. No black cap.

Black cap

The male is bright yellow in summer, olive-green in winter

Juveniles look like an adult female

White rump

Black tail is notched

"Po-ta-to-chip!" means "This is my space!" (Sounds like a squeeze-toy.)

Leap Froggin' Goldfinch

Cold, wind, ice and snow send many birds packing their feathers and heading south for the winter. They are looking for warmth and food. American Goldfinches stay. They have adapted to Michigan's chilly winters and the change from the large food supply of summer to a limited winter store of seeds. In fact, they can make winter feeding look like a group game! Taking turns in leap frog fashion over mass seed sources is an efficient (energy-saving and safe) way for goldfinches to feed in large winter flocks. This rolling motion over a field helps to protect the flock from predators. Your turn!

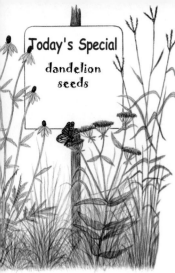

Today's Special
dandelion seeds

Habitat Café

Yumm . . . bring an order of thistle seed and spring tree buds salted with aphids. Fill your backyard bird feeder with Nyjer thistle seed. American Goldfinches are granivores. They use cone-shaped bill used to break open seeds.

SPRING, SUMMER, FALL, WINTER MENU:

 Mostly seeds, a few insects

Life Cycle

NEST The female builds the cup-shaped nest, 2–20 feet above the ground in the fork of thistle, a shrub or a deciduous tree. With spider silk, she weaves a nest base to the support branches. Next, rootlets are woven in. Soft thistle down is added last. The nest is so compact (tight), it can hold water like a cup!

EGGS About ½ inch long. The female incubates the 4–6 eggs for 12–14 days. The male feeds her regurgitated (spit-up) food from his crop. Gross, but it works!

MOM! DAD! Altricial. Both Mom and Dad feed the young. For the first four days Dad feeds Mom, and then she feeds the chicks.

NESTLING Feathers replace the chick's down when they are about one week old, nearly the time they are ready to leave the nest.

FLEDGLING Young goldfinches continue to be cared for by the male for three more weeks. They can then forage for seeds on their own.

JUVENILE Juveniles group with other goldfinches and move to areas with plenty of food. In one year, they can nest and raise their own chicks.

Did You Know

Most parent birds feed their young a diet of high-protein insects. American Goldfinches feed their young seeds. When Brown-headed Cowbirds lay their eggs in the nest of a goldfinch, the cowbird chicks die (see the Baltimore Oriole on page 82 about cowbird habits). The seed diet does not have enough protein for cowbird chicks to live. The goldfinch chicks then have the full attention of their parents.

When
The American Goldfinch is diurnal. It feeds during the day and rests at night.

Migration
Permanent resident to short distance migrant. The American Goldfinch may move to central and southern regions of the U.S. during harsh winters. Many stay in Michigan during the winter as year-round backyard visitors.

Nesting
One of Michigan's latest nesting begins in July. When the thistle and milkweed down is mature and fluffy, it is time for goldfinch nesting in Michigan.

Getting Around
The male flies in spiral circles over the nesting area. He sings his most impressive, 'po-ta-to-chip.' Two or three males join, each circling in crisscross paths like fluttering bright-yellow butterflies. Biologists call this behavior a Butterfly Flight Pattern.

Where to Look
Open grassland, rural fields and native prairies, shrub edges and backyards throughout most of Michigan.

| Year-round | Summer |
| Migration | Winter |

Savannah Sparrow

Passerculus sandwichensis

Length: 4 ½–6 inches
Wingspan: 6 ½ inches

Gray bill

Crown has pale stripe in the middle

Throat and belly white

Yellow eyebrow stripe

Neck, nape, back and rump are brown-gray with streaks

Breast streaked with white spot in center

Pink legs

"Buzzz" Males sing a short, insect-like buzzing song during breeding season to attract a gal.

Scamper, Crouch, Zigzag and Chase

Savannah Sparrow survival lessons may follow like this: In your five flight plans the main pattern is short, low and rapid. Use this to patrol your territory. When in danger employ the drop to the ground tactic. Then, with both wings raised, scamper zigzag along the ground. In all other ground action crouch and imitate a mouse. Parents, approach the nest with a direct flight and hover before swiftly dropping to the nest. Guys, guard the nest at all cost and use your flutter flight to threaten intruders. Keep your legs dangling, tail cocked at 45° and wings beating in a constant flutter. If a predator is another male Savannah Sparrow, open full bore and chase it with all you have!

Today's Special
beetles
butterflies

Habitat Café

Yumm... bring an order of insects and a small fruit salad sprinkled with seeds. Savannah Sparrows are omnivorous. Using its strong beak, the sparrow crushes an insect, shakes or strikes it against the ground. It then swallows a non-squirmy meal.

SPRING, SUMMER, MENU:
 Mostly insects

FALL, WINTER MENU:
 Small seeds, fruits, some insects

Life Cycle

NEST The female builds the 3-inch diameter cup nest on the ground hidden in tall, dead grasses. The outer shell has coarse grass and the inner shell is made of soft, fine grass.

EGGS About ¾ inch long. The female incubates the clutch of 2-6 (4 average) eggs for 14–16 days.

MOM! DAD! Altricial. During the chicks early 8-day growth spurt, Mom needs to eat nearly 10 times her body mass to keep pace. It takes a great deal of energy to catch and carry family meals. She can multi-task and carry 10-20 small prey (midges) in a trip, but caterpillars have to carried one-by-one.

NESTLINGS Both parents help with diaper duty and provide insects and spiders for the chicks' bottomless appetites.

FLEDGLING At 11-12 days of age, the young leave the nest.

JUVENILE Before their first migration, they group into loose flocks of just 3-8 individuals or a party of 100.

Unsolved Mystery

How do Savannah Sparrows determine their nightly flight route during fall and spring migration? The setting sun is the GPS (Global Positioning System) for these grassland sparrows. It is used as a source of day-to-day mapping information. This information may be then transferred to the stars as celestial reference points each night. Bird migration still has mysteries just waiting to be solved.

When

Diurnal. Savannah Sparrows are active during the day and rest at night.

Migration

Spring Arrival: mid-April
Fall Departure: Aug–Sept
Short to long-distance migrant to central and southern United States and as far south as Mexico and the Honduras.

Nesting

Savannah Sparrows begin nesting in May–June in Michigan.

Getting Around

Savannah Sparrows walk on the ground to capture prey. Their main foes include the stealthy Northern Harriers and American Kestrels.

Where to Look

Michigan's grasslands, hayfields and pastures, meadows and grassy marshes. The Savannah Sparrow is more common in Michigan's southern LP.

Year-round	Summer
Migration	Winter

Bobolink

Dolichonyx oryzivorus

Length: 6–8 inches
Wingspan: 11–12 inches

female

Female is buff color with streaks down her back, wings and sides

The male wears a backwards tuxedo, with a black belly, wings and head set off by white on his back; he is also nicknamed the "skunk bird"

Juveniles look like females without streaks on the side and more yellow underneath

Stiff, pointed tail feathers

"Bob-o-link, bob-o-link, sspink, spank, sspink." Males, "This is my space. Gals, come over."

Drawing the Line

Male Bobolinks decide where their space (territory) begins and the neighboring male's space ends by doing a boogie called the "Parallel Walk." First they show off their most colorful marking, the yellow patch on the back of the neck. They turn their head down and to the side. Next, the two neighbors hop side by side along an invisible line. This boogie-woogie can go on for hours. "Hey, you're on my side of the line!" Reminds me of the invisible line my sister had down the middle of the back seat in the family car.

Today's Special
caterpillars

Habitat Café

Yumm . . . bring an order of spiders, beetles, grasshoppers and crickets. As they migrate, Bobolinks eat large amounts of grain in the "milk" stage. This creates body fat (energy reserves) for the long flight south.

SPRING, SUMMER, FALL MENU:
 Mainly insects, lots of seeds and grains

WINTER MENU:
 Almost all seeds and grains, some insects

Life Cycle

NEST The female builds the nest in an open field. She picks up grasses and builds them around a low area on the ground. Next, she lines the nest with soft, fine grasses.

EGGS About ⅝ inch long. The female incubates the 5–6 eggs for 12–13 days.

MOM! DAD! Altricial. Mom does most of the parenting. Dad has up to four hungry families full of hatchlings at the same time.

NESTLING The newly hatched chicks are naked. They grow feathers by the time they are 10 days old and leave the nest.

FLEDGLING Feathers that are the same color as the ground help hide the fledglings in a field or prairie. They can fly on their own at about 2 weeks of age. They beg for food from their parents until they are 3–4 weeks old.

JUVENILE Juveniles join in a flock with their family group and get ready for fall migration. When they return in the spring, they are mature enough to date, mate and raise their own young.

Did You Know

Eggs are laid one per day over 5–6 days, but all hatch within a day or two of each other. Biologists designed experiments to find out how the eggs might be different depending on what day in the line-up they were laid. Eggs laid last had more of a body chemical called testosterone than the eggs laid first. Higher levels of testosterone cause faster growth and more aggressiveness, helping the chicks from the last eggs catch up!

When
Bobolinks are diurnal. They migrate by night in large flocks and rest by day.

Migration
Spring Arrival: late April–May
Fall Departure: Aug –Sept
Long-distance migrant. The Bobolink makes one of the longest migrations of any North American songbird, winging deep into South America, where it spends the winter in "pampas" grass of Brazil and Argentina—it's an 11,000-mile round trip!

Nesting
Bobolinks begin nesting in Michigan in May.

Getting Around
Bobolinks walk slowly while pecking seeds and insects. Flight during nesting season is fast and low, to keep out of the sight of hungry predators. Long hind toenails allow Bobolinks to perch on plant stems.

Where to Look
Open grassland and rural fields over most of Michigan with larger numbers in the LP. Prefer native prairies but have adapted to hay fields of at least 1–5 acres in size.
· Dansville State Game Area
· Seven Ponds Nature Center
· Port Huron State Game Area

Year-round   Summer
Migration   Winter

Horned Lark

Eremophila alpestris

Length: 7 inches
Wingspan: 12 inches

horns

Black patch on side of head and a black band across forehead

The "horns" are tufts of black feathers

Juveniles do not have the black head and throat markings of the adult. "Horns" are formed by two years of age.

White or yellow throat

Females look like males with a duller color

Black patch on breast

Black tail with white on the sides

"Su-weet!" This sweet song is sung from a perch like a fencepost or shrub.

Aerobatic Antics

Beginning as early as February in Michigan, the male Horned Lark begins his airborne "impress the ladies" show. Singing while he flies in a sky-bound spiral, he climbs higher and higher until he is lost in the clouds. Closing his wings, he plunges headfirst toward the prairie. Then, nearly scraping the ground, he opens his wings, turns and climbs skyward to perform his daring display all over again. He hopes the female Horned Larks are wowed, awed and rendered totally chirpless.

Habitat Café

Yumm . . . bring an order of small weed seeds, hold the onions, please. Adult Horned Larks eat mostly seeds with a few insects, and are omnivores. They feed protein-rich insects to their chicks for fast growth.

SPRING, SUMMER, FALL MENU:
Mostly seeds, some insects

WINTER MENU:
More seeds and fewer insects than during spring, summer and fall

Life Cycle

NEST The female builds the nest beginning with a shallow dip in the ground, near or under grass. She makes a nest cup with stems and leaves, lining it with fine grasses.

EGGS About ⅝ inch long. The female incubates the 3–5 pale, grayish white eggs for 11 days.

MOM! DAD! Altricial. Both Mom and Dad help feed the young. On average, a very young chick can expect food once every 5–6 minutes. Their eyes open when they are 4 days old.

NESTLING The chicks hatch with a downy covering, ready for the chilly, early spring temperatures.

FLEDGLING Young Horned Larks leave the nest at 10 days old, when they have their primary feathers. They can walk and fly like an adult when they are about one month of age.

JUVENILE Juvenile larks gather in small groups throughout the summer, go through their first molt (old feathers fall out and new feathers grow in) and prepare to migrate.

Unsolved Mystery

Female Horned Larks have been seen placing small pebbles on one side of the nest rim. Are they building a nest patio? Are the pebbles a way to hold down the grasses while she works on the nest? Use your scientific detective skills to find the answer to this unsolved mystery!

When

Horned Larks are diurnal. They feed during the day and rest at night.

Migration

Spring Arrival: March–April
Fall Departure: Dec.–Jan.
The Horned Lark is a short distance migrant that moves to central, southern and southeastern regions of the U.S. Some Horned Larks may remain in Michigan in winter when little snow covers their food source, the grains in open fields.

Nesting

Horned Larks get a jump on the season, nesting as early as March in Michigan, even while there is snow cover; 1–3 broods per year are possible.

Getting Around

Horned Larks forage (look for food) on the ground in crop fields, gravel roadsides and in fields and prairies of short grasses. In flight, their wings beat 3–4 times; then are folded against the body for 1–2 beats.

Where to Look

Open agricultural areas across Michigan, especially in the southern LP.
· Fletcher Plains

| Year-round | Summer |
| Migration | Winter |

American Kestrel

Falco sparverius

Length: 9 inches
Wingspan: 20–24 inches

Black-and-white
face pattern

Markings on the back of
the head look like a pair of
false eyes or "ocelli"

female

Females have red-brown
wings and seven to nine
dark bands across the tail.
Brown-streaked breast.
Female larger than male.

Hooked,
sharp beak

Narrow body,
long tail

Juveniles look like
adults with dull colors

"Killy, killy, killy"
means
"Stay away!"

Build and They Will Come

Build a kestrel nest box and place it on a tree or a pole near a grassy area with small mammals, insects
and a few snakes for good measure, and these small falcons may come. In Michigan, both kestrel nesting
boxes and trees with hollow cavities found along the edges of open areas provide important structures
for kestrels. Be involved. Build a nest box for kestrels. Ask your Audubon club for the best place to hang
a nest box. Include a hinged lid to carefully check the inside of the box during nesting season and keep
a record of the number of eggs, young and adults. Make an older tree in your yard a wildlife tree and
watch these handy neighbors as they eat unwelcome insects and rodents!

Today's Special
ground
squirrels

Habitat Café

Yumm . . . bring an order of mice, snakes, lizards, caterpillars, beetles, dragonflies, crickets and a few small birds and animals. American Kestrels are carnivorous. Kestrel parents plan for the kids' extra snacks and poor weather conditions by caching uneaten prey in grass clumps, tree roots, holes and limbs, or a fence post.

SPRING, SUMMER, FALL MENU:
Mostly insects, some birds and animals

WINTER MENU:
All small animals

Life Cycle

NEST Kestrels prefer to nest in a woodpecker hole or natural tree cavity at the edge of a wooded area. With the loss of nesting habitat, they have adapted to using nest boxes near their food. They do not bring in nesting materials but may add feathers. A few wood chips may be placed in the bottom of a nest box.

EGGS About 1⅛ inches long. The female incubates the 4–5 eggs for 30 days. The male takes over when the female leaves for a short time each day. Both have a "brood patch," an area on the belly without feathers. Putting a bare belly to eggs keeps them warm.

MOM! DAD! Altricial. Both Mom and Dad help feed the young.

NESTLING The brown-gray chicks stay in the nest for 30 days. Young kestrels shoot their feces (body wastes) onto the upper walls of the nest cavity. The bottom of the nest stays fairly clean.

FLEDGLING Parents feed the young for the first two weeks after they leave the nest.

JUVENILE The first year is the hardest for birds to survive. According to research, only 4 out of 10 kestrels reach their first birthday.

Gross Factor

How do some bird species determine the most productive hunting areas? By seeing the urine trails left by their prey. The urine of voles and other small mammals contain nitrogen components (chemical parts) that reflect and fluoresce ultraviolet (UV) light. Many birds, but not people, can see UV light and can detect the small mammal runways marked by urine along the ground!

When
American Kestrels are diurnal. They feed during the day and rest at night.

Migration
Spring Arrival: March
Fall Departure: Aug–Sept
Short to long distance migrant. Some kestrels stay year-round in southern LP or until snow covers the ground and prey is hard to find. Some migrate as far south as Mexico and Panama.

Nesting
American Kestrels nest in April in Michigan.

Getting Around
Kestrels hover in one place by facing into the wind with their wings spread. Their boomerang-shaped wings have a notch in the outer three primary feathers to aid in hovering. The tail is used as a rudder to steady the bird while it searches for prey below. Kestrels perch on utility lines and poles and look for prey.

Where to Look
Most of Michigan (except deep forested regions) along highways, railroad tracks, rural roadsides, pastures and open fields.
· Fort Custer Recreation Area

Year-round   Summer
Migration   Winter

Eastern Kingbird

Tyrannus tyrannus

Length: 8 inches
Wingspan: 15 inches

Black head with hidden red "king's" crown. When excited, the male raises his head feathers to show off his crown.

White chin

Gray on top with a white belly and underside

Males, females and juveniles look very much alike

Black tail with white band

"Chatter-zeer" could be "Hi. I'm back." Or a male telling others that he's patrolling his territory.

Tyrant of the Air

Tyrants are bullies. *Tyrannosaurus rex* dinosaurs are thought to have bullied other dinosaurs earlier in earth's history. *Tyrannus tyrannus*, the Eastern Kingbird, is known today for bullying bigger birds to claim its territory and protect its young. If a hawk, crow or owl flies even 100 feet above an Eastern Kingbird nest, watch out. The kingbird will mount a full aerial attack that includes chasing and crashing into the bigger bird from above while screeching, *Zeeeer!* The predator is . . . out of there.

Today's Special
fresh wasps

Habitat Café

Yumm . . . bring an order of dragonflies, drone bumblebees, beetles and grasshoppers. Eastern Kingbirds are omnivorous. They feed on insects in Michigan and fruits in their South American wintering grounds.

SPRING, SUMMER, FALL MENU:
 Almost entirely insects, some berries

WINTER MENU:
 Mostly fruit, a few insects

Life Cycle

NEST The female builds the messy, but sturdy, nest 10–20 feet above the ground with plant stems and small twigs on a tree limb. She lines the nest with soft cottonwood or cattail down.

EGGS About ¾ inch long. The female incubates the clutch of 3–4 eggs for 14–16 days.

MOM! DAD! Altricial. Both Mom and Dad help feed the young.

NESTLING The chicks hatch naked with orange skin and their eyes closed. After the first day, the colorful skin changes to gray and feathers begin to form.

FLEDGLING The young normally leave the nest when they are able to fly weakly, at about 2½ weeks. The parents kill the prey, mostly flying insects, and remove the stingers from bees and wasps before feeding them to the young. Ouch! What parents will do for their kids!

JUVENILE Juveniles stay in the family group until just before fall migration. They are ready to date, mate and raise their own young when they return to Michigan in the spring.

Did You Know

Kingbirds wait on their perch for a flying insect to come near. They snatch it from the air in a short, quick flight called "hawking." How does a bird overcome gravity to fly? How does it fly against "drag," the resistance of the air flowing over its body in flight? Wing shape and physics. If you haven't studied flight yet, turn to page 194 for a wing up on lift and Bernoulli's Principle.

When

Eastern Kingbirds are diurnal. They feed during the day and rest at night.

Migration

Spring Arrival: May
Fall Departure: Aug–Sept
Long-distance migrant. Migrate during the day in flocks of 10–60 birds to Central and South America, as far as Peru and Argentina.

Nesting

Eastern Kingbirds begin nesting in May–June in Michigan.

Getting Around

Perch on plants, fence posts or branches. The male does a "tumble flight." First, he flies high in a fluttering flight. Next, in short glides and aerobatic tumbles, he falls to the earth, Red Baron style. Good grief!

Where to Look

Most of Michigan along roadsides, grasslands, prairies and fields. Look for Eastern Kingbirds perched on dead branches along Michigan lakes while you're fishing for bass, panfish, or a toothy northern pike.
· Fort Custer Recreation Area

Year-round   Summer
Migration   Winter

Prairie and Open Grasslands Habitat

Eastern Meadowlark

Sturnella magna

Length: 9 inches
Wingspan: 14 inches

in flight

Slender bill

Males are larger and females are not as brightly colored

Black V (bib) on chest

Bright yellow breast and belly

Short tail with white edges in flight

Long legs and toes

3-5 flute-like whistles slurred together sliding high to low, "See you at school soon!"

Woolly Mammoths and Meadowlarks

What do they have in common? Fossil records show that they both lived in North America over 10,000 years ago. Woolly Mammoths are extinct; there are no more Woolly Mammoths living on earth. Meadowlarks are still here, but with continued habitat loss, their numbers continue to fall. Male Eastern Meadowlarks use 7–8 acres of grassland for their breeding territory (space). What can you do? In rural Michigan, set aside a large grassy area free of chemicals and predators. Wait to mow, hay, or graze the area until after nesting season. Include a tall post for a meadowlark to stretch its bill to the sky and sing. Set up your spotting scope. Watch and listen for a new black-bibbed neighbor!

Today's Special
crickets

Habitat Café

Yumm . . . bring an order of crickets, grasshoppers and seeds with a side order of wild fruits. Eastern Meadowlarks are omnivorous and eat plant and animal matter. They probe for grubs and worms by "gaping" (putting their closed, pointed bill in the ground and opening it).

SPRING, SUMMER, FALL MENU:
 Mostly insects, some seeds and fruit

WINTER MENU:
 Weed seeds, field grains (corn) and some wild fruits

Life Cycle

NEST The female builds a dome-like nest in a grassy field. A deep spot in the ground is filled with large grasses and then lined with fine, soft grasses. A dome is built over the top by weaving together plants growing around the nest. An opening is left on one side of the nest with a path through the grass for coming and going.

EGGS About 1 inch long. The female incubates the 2–6 eggs for 13–14 days. If the nest is disturbed, the female will leave and not go back to incubate the eggs. Respect the need for safe nesting.

MOM! DAD! Altricial. Mom does most of the feeding. Dad does not go to the nest. He may catch insects and 'beak' them over to Mom.

NESTLING Nestlings need to eat more than half of their body weight in food each day. Mom averages 100 trips per day to gather insects for her famished brood.

FLEDGLING With long, quick legs and the ability to hide in plants, the young leave the nest at about 1½ weeks of age. Their parents feed them for two more weeks, until they can fly.

JUVENILE They look like their parents but with spots instead of a black bib on their chest. In one year, they are mature enough to nest.

Did You Know

Each meadowlark male has his own large (up to 80 or more) collection of songs. Meadowlarks learn songs during a specific period of time when they are young. If they do not hear the song of an Eastern Meadowlark during this window of learning, they will adopt a song from another bird species. Eastern Meadowlarks have even taken on the song of a Northern Cardinal!

When

Meadowlarks are diurnal. They feed during the day and rest at night.

Migration
Spring Arrival March–April
Fall Departure Oct–Nov
Short to long distance migrant. Spend winter in areas with temperatures above 10 degrees, as far south as Mexico. In spring, males arrive 2–4 weeks ahead of females to set up territories.

Nesting
Eastern Meadowlarks begin nesting in April–May in Michigan.

Getting Around
Meadowlarks walk and run on the ground. When a female meadowlark nears her nest, she walks closer to the ground to hide from predators. Their flight is a glide followed by quick wing beats. They can fly 20–40 miles per hour.

Where to Look
Open grasslands and rural uncropped fields, prairies, and grassy roadsides. More commonly in Michigan's LP.
· Sharonville State Game Area
· Dansville State Game Area

Year-round   Summer
Migration   Winter

**Prairie and Open
Grasslands Habitat**

129

Killdeer

Charadrius vociferus

Length: 9–11 inches
Wingspan: 24 inches

injury-feigning display

The downy young and juveniles have only one black band across their breast

Olive-brown

Rusty orange rump patch is seen when tail is spread

Both the male and the female have two black bands across their breast

White underside

Long legs for wading in the shallow water and running fast

"Kill—deer, kill—deer!" or "Sound the alarm! Danger near!"

Best Drama Award

The Killdeer spread out and crushed on the ground in front of you looks like a dying bird uttering it last painful, *dee*. Bringing itself from sure death, the Killdeer limps along with a broken wing. Watch it long enough and the wing may suddenly heal. Poor bird? Smart, tricky bird that has just lured predator away from its young by pretending to be injured. This behavior is called an "injury-feignin display." The Killdeer fakes an injury to protect its young. Your part in this drama is that of a respon sible neighbor. Watch the nesting area from afar with a spotting scope or binoculars. Your reward wi be more Killdeer to watch in the future. Take a bow.

130

Today's Special
crayfish

Habitat Café

Yumm . . . bring an order grasshoppers, beetles, earthworms, ticks, and mosquito larvae with a side of Green Treefrog. Killdeer are omnivorous.

SPRING, SUMMER, FALL MENU:
 Mostly insects, crustaceans and amphibians, some seeds

WINTER MENU:
 Entirely insects and crustaceans

Life Cycle

NEST The nest is a simple, low scrape in the ground. It is lined with pebbles, gravel or woodchips that help keep the eggs from rolling away with wind and rain. They will also nest in flat rooftops and in gravel parking lots.

EGGS About 1½ inches long. Both the male and female incubate the 4 camouflaged eggs for 24–25 days. Killdeer eggs fit together tightly with the pointed end to the center. This helps the eggs stay warm and keep from rolling away.

MOM! DAD! Precocial. Parents do not feed the chicks. As soon as the chicks have hatched and their down is dry, the parents lead them to feeding areas. Parents brood the young for the first few days and guard them for the first ten days. Chicks can swim across small streams.

FLEDGLING If a predator comes near, chicks lay low and freeze. Some will raise their legs above the grass to look like a stem or stick. Killdeer stay with their parents and siblings until they can fly at 3–4 weeks of age.

JUVENILE Killdeer can nest and mate when they are one year of age.

Did You Know?

Nesting on a rooftop can be dangerous. Killdeer in this situation can be creative when it is time to lead their newly hatched chicks to food. One pair of Killdeer parents called to their chicks from the ground near the base of a rain gutter. The chicks heard the parents call to come down from the roof and they used the rain-spout as a slide.

When

Killdeer are diurnal. They feed during the day and rest at night. Migrate by day and night.

Migration

Spring Arrival: Feb–March
Fall Departure: Late Sept.–Nov. Long-distance migrant. Killdeer migrate south in flocks of up to 30 birds to Central and South America. They are one of the first spring arrivals to Michigan.

Nesting

Killdeer nest in Michigan beginning in April.

Getting Around

Killdeer have a standard ground move: run a short ways, stop, bob their head and run again. They keep their body straight while their long legs are a blur of motion. In flight, they are strong and fast at speeds of 28–35 miles per hour. Adult Killdeer can swim in fast-flowing water.

Where to Look

Originally a shorebird found on mud flats and sandbars, the Killdeer has adapted to open habitats: fields, grazed pastures, golf courses, gravel parking lots, flat rooftops, soccer fields, airports and playgrounds.
· Super Adaptor

Year-round | Summer
Migration | Winter

Prairie and Open Grasslands Habitat

Sharp-tailed Grouse

Tympanuchus phasianellus

Length: 16–18 1/2 inches
Wingspan: 25 inches

female

Males and females are similar with males heavier

White under-tail

Head, neck, back and wings barred with brown, black and buff

Round body with short legs

During courtship displays, the male puffs out his eye combs and purple neck sacs

Orange/yellow eye "combs"

Feathered nostril and legs

White upper belly marked with small dark V's

"Up-up-up" Both females and males give this call when taking flight. Males have six calls to attract females. Her favorite is his 'bottle cork popping' sound.

Heartbeat of the Open Grasslands

The ground thumped and drummed. The air echoed clicks, cackles, coos and tail rattles. Arch-winged birds with ballooned orange brows and purple neck sacs circled invisible territories and battled for mere inches. Sharp-tailed Grouse have been performing this song and dance in the early morning each spring since about 1920 on Michigan's northern open grass and shrub lands. Male leks, or courtship sites, are 40 acres of open area for dancing, with another surrounding 320 acres for nesting and feeding. Visit Seney National Wildlife Refuge and other protected areas they still call home and witness this heartbeat of the grasslands firsthand.

Habitat Café

Yumm... bring an order of seeds, buds, insects and fruits with side orders of plants and flowers. Sharp-tailed Grouse are omnivorous. Food is often stored in their crop for digesting later. Once in the crop, food is ground into smaller pieces by small stones and chokecherry seeds—internal "teeth".

SPRING, SUMMER MENU:

 Mostly insects, plants and fruit

FALL, WINTER MENU:

Seeds, buds, plants and fruit

Life Cycle

NEST The female makes the oval ground nest in thick plants and grasses, or under a shrub or small tree. The outer nest of grass, sedges, leaves, and moss is lined with finer grasses and her soft feathers.

EGGS About ¾ inch long. The female incubates the clutch of 10–12 eggs for 21–23 days.

MOM! DAD! Precocial. The chicks hatch with downy feathers and their eyes fully open. They follow Mom and leave the nest to feed on their own. She protects the chicks from sun, rain and cold for the first few days. By 8 weeks of age, they are half the size of an adult, and by 12 weeks, full adult size. Everyone in this brood is on the lookout for predators: red fox, coyote, mink, Red-tailed Hawks and the stealth planes of the open grasslands, Northern Harriers.

JUVENILE The young stay close to the nest during the summer but come September, the family members part. Young males may get a jump on the dating season and scout possible spring territories. They may practice battling with rushes, face-offs, stand-offs and pecking.

History Hangout

The first native dancers on Michigan's open grasslands and prairies were the Greater Prairie Chickens, cousins to the Sharp-tailed Grouse. With the changing land use in the 1900s, the large expanses of native prairies needed by the Prairie Chickens were gone and so were they by 1981. The Michigan DNR and private groups like the Michigan Sharp-tailed Grouse Association are working together to keep Sharp-tails from the same fate. Keep on dancing in northern Michigan, Sharp-tails!

When

Diurnal. Sharp-tailed Grouse are active during the day and rest at night.

Migration

Permanent resident. Sharp-tailed Grouse remain in Michigan all year. In winters with heavy snow, they may move to woody habitats for food and cover.

Nesting

Sharp-tailed Grouse begin nesting in May–June in Michigan.

Getting Around

Sharp-tailed Grouse travel short distances in a flight of 3 rapid wing-beats and then a glide. They walk on the ground and "flight hop" from branch to branch. Their pectinae (fleshy knobs on their toes) grow longer and more numerous in the winter. This allows them to walk on the snow, as if they were wearing snowshoes.

Where to Look

Found in the open grass and shrublands of Michigan's UP and west central LP.

· Seney National Wildlife Refuge
· Hiawatha NF
· Escanaba River SF

Year-round   Summer
Migration   Winter

Northern Harrier

Circus cyaneus

Length: 16–24 inches
Wingspan: 3½–4 feet

wheeling

White rump patch

Males are silver gray above and lighter below

female

The females are brown above and cream and brown streaked below, with a banded tail

Black wingtips

Juveniles look similar to females but are darker brown above and russet below

"Kek, kek, kek" means "Stay away!"

Long, square tail

Flying Food Pass

Watch Northern Harriers during the summer. Watch closely. You may see the male perform a flying food pass. When he has a juicy mouse, he signals to the female on the nest below, "purrduk." She flies just under him, turns over and catches the mouse in her talons. A speedy delivery is made to the hungry chicks. Keep watch for Northern Harriers to pick up a mouse nest, shake it, then drop the nest. A litter of young mice and their parents are snatched up for a quick snack. How do they know the nest is full of mice? As they glide over Michigan's grassy fields and prairies, harriers hear prey before they see it with a facial disk that funnels sound to their enlarged ear openings.

Today's Special
gophers

Habitat Café

Yumm . . . Bring an order of mice, voles, shrews, frogs, lizards and small perching birds. Northern Harriers are carnivorous. They eat only animal matter. When their main prey, meadow voles, increase in great numbers in a given year, the number of young harriers produced increases. Supply side food economics!

SPRING, SUMMER, FALL, WINTER MENU:

 Entirely animal matter

Life Cycle

NEST The female builds a pile of grass and weeds on the ground, hollowed in the top with a few sticks or twigs as the base.

EGGS About 1¾ inches long. The female incubates 4–6 eggs for 30 days. The male brings her food and may shade or guard the eggs while she takes a break.

MOM! DAD! Altricial. Dad brings the food to Mom. She feeds the chicks by tearing the food into pieces as they take it from her bill. Unlike their quiet parents, the chicks use noisy screech calls to scare predators.

NESTLING When a chick strays from the nest, Mom carries it back home in her bill by the nape (back of neck). After two weeks of age, the young take paths through the grass to raised feeding and resting areas.

FLEDGLING As heavy as an adult, they can fly at one month of age and their meals come in an aerial pass from their parents. To practice capturing prey, the young pounce on objects on the ground.

JUVENILE Juveniles join with others their age, feeding and preparing for migration. It takes 2–3 years to gain their adult plumage and be mature enough to raise their own young.

Birding Tip

LOOK OUT OVERHEAD! These strong birds of prey will dive at and possibly even sink their talons into anyone that gets close to the nest. It's a good idea not to disturb the nest or nesting area during this sensitive time. Adults may abandon the young and you may be in danger. Safety first, for everyone!

When

Northern Harriers are diurnal. They can spend 40 percent of their day in flight, logging up to 100 miles per day!

Migration

Spring Arrival: March–May
Fall Departure: late August–Nov
Long-distance migrant. Flying alone, they migrate to Texas, Mexico, Costa Rica and Panama.

Nesting

The only ground nesting hawk in the state, Northern Harriers begin nesting in April–May in Michigan.

Getting Around

Look for Northern Harriers in an open field flying low (10–13 feet) over the ground with their slim, lightweight body, and long wings. They fly with a series of flaps and tilting glides, their wings held in a spread-out V. Their outer 3-5 primary flight feathers are notched for aerodynamic soaring.

Where to Look

Undisturbed grasslands, native prairies, inland and coastal wetlands in Michigan.
· Lake Erie Metropark– migration
· Munuscong WMA
· Wigwam Bay Wildlife Area

Year-round   Summer
Migration   Winter

Red-tailed Hawk

Buteo jamaicensis

Length: 18–25 inches
Wingspan: 4–5 feet

soaring

Dark head and upper side, lighter underside

White underside with brown streaks on belly that may resemble a band

Male and female look the same, but the female is larger, stronger

Tail is "red" on upper side with a narrow, dark band

Only adult hawks have red tails

"Kee-eee-arr!" or, "This is my territory."

Migration Skyways

Tens of thousands of birds move along the migratory skyway over the shores of the Great Lakes in Sept.-Nov. and again March-May. From Whitefish Point, Keweenaw Peninsula, Lake Erie Metropark, Pointe Mouillee, the Straits of Mackinaw, Port Huron and Manitou Island you can view Red-tailed Hawks and other raptors, as well as shorebirds, waterfowl, and songbirds on the move. You don't have to wait until migration to see Red-tailed Hawks. Their rust-colored tails flash overhead from spring through fall (some all year) and they have become more common along rural and urban roadways. Look for red-tails perched on power lines, in trees, and on billboards scanning roadside ditches for a meal of rabbit and rodents.

Today's Special
muskrats

Habitat Café

Yumm . . . bring an order of rabbits, mice, voles, chipmunks, squirrels, snakes, gophers, skinks and pheasants. Red-tailed Hawks are carnivorous. Sharp, hooked beak and talons are used for capturing and tearing apart prey. Taken to a feeding perch, small mammals are swallowed whole and birds are beheaded, plucked and eaten. Bill-licking good.

SPRING, SUMMER, FALL, WINTER MENU:
 Mostly mammals, some reptiles, birds and amphibians

Life Cycle

NEST The male and female build the bulky nest in a large tree, 30–90 feet from the ground. They may return to the same nest for several years, adding more sticks and lining it with moss, evergreen twigs and grapevine bark. Nests that are reused for years can be over three feet deep!

EGGS Slightly more than 2¼ inches long. The female and male incubate the 2–3, dull, creamy white eggs for 28–35 days.

MOM! DAD! Altricial. Both Mom and Dad feed the young. At first the parents tear off pieces of prey for the chicks, but as they grow, the parents leave the food for the young to tear apart on their own. Learning to be independent is a big deal in the bird world!

NESTLING Fluffy down begins to be replaced by new feathers when the chicks are about two weeks of age.

FLEDGLING Young Red-tailed Hawks leave the nest and fly when they are 6–7 weeks old.

JUVENILE Immature hawks have a gray-brown tail with dark bands. It takes two years to develop the red tail. Immature Red-tailed Hawks begin to migrate south before the adults in the fall.

Unsolved Mystery

Red-tailed Hawks put a fresh, leafy branch in the nest with the chicks every day. Why? To shade the young? To hide the young from predators? Do the aromatic oils in the leaves help control parasites on the chicks' skin? To solve this mystery use a spotting scope from far away. Parent hawks will not go near the nest if they suspect it is being watched.

When

Red-tailed Hawks are diurnal, feeding during the day and resting at night.

Migration

Spring Arrival: March–May
Fall departure: Sept–Nov
Permanent resident in southern Michigan while some migrate to the southern U.S. and Mexico during the winter months.

Nesting

Red-tailed Hawks begin egg laying in April in Michigan.

Getting Around

Red-tailed Hawks soar, perch and fly low to the ground to find prey with their keen eyesight. Once they spot it, they dive or pounce on their prey, carrying it away in their strong talons. Look high in the sky for a soaring Red-tailed Hawk with its tail and wings spread out, seemingly motionless.

Where to Look

Red-tailed Hawks prefer open areas with large trees nearby for perching but also hunt for prey along both rural and urban roadsides throughout Michigan.
· *Super Adaptor*
· Leelanau State Park - migration
· West Bloomfield Woods Nature Preserve

Year-round   Summer
Migration   Winter

Ring-necked Pheasant

Phasianus colchicus

Length: 23–30 inches
Wingspan: 31 inches

female

Red around eye

Iridescent green and
purple feathers on head
and neck

The female is smaller than
the male and brown. She
blends in with the ground.
Shorter, brown tail.

White collar

Long, pointed tail

A spur on back of the
male's legs is for defense
during territorial fights
with other males

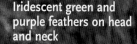
"Koork - kok!"
The male crowing,
"This is my territory."

Birds From Afar

Originally a native of Asia, the Ring-necked Pheasant was successfully introduced to Michigan in 1918, and was a common sight in rural farming areas by the 1930s. Today, it is one of the most popular game bird species in Michigan (a bird that can be legally hunted for food and sport). The Michigan DNR keeps track of the pheasant population. During late July–early August, selected rural mail carriers in southern Michigan record the number of pheasant broods, chicks and hens on their mail route. Hunters can help the DNR by recording the number of pheasants flushed per hour of hunting. Working together to ensure a future for wildlife in Michigan can be great fun!

Today's Winter Special

shrub buds

Habitat Café

Yumm . . . bring an order of seeds, grasses, leaves, roots, wild fruits, nuts and insects. Pheasants are omnivores. Females eat more insects, shells and snails during the nesting season for the calcium needed to make eggs.

SPRING, SUMMER, FALL MENU:
Lots of seeds, some insects

WINTER MENU:
More seeds and fewer insects than during spring, summer and fall

Life Cycle

NEST The female builds the nest in tall grasses. She finds a deep spot in the ground and pulls in the grasses around her body.

EGGS About 1¾ inches long. The female incubates the 6–15 eggs for 23–25 days.

MOM! DAD! Precocial. With downy feathers, eyes open and legs well developed, the chicks follow Mom out of the nest within hours of hatching. Young pheasants are able to fly short distances by the time they are a week old.

During the first six weeks, chicks find and eat the largest insects they can fit in their mouth and swallow! The chicks add more plants and seeds to their diet as they grow.

JUVENILE Juveniles stay in the area with their Mom until they are about 10 weeks of age. They are mature enough to date, mate and raise their own chicks at one year of age.

Did You Know?

One of the most important jobs of a parent bird during incubation is turning the eggs. Eggshells have tiny holes for the exchange of air, gases and water vapor important to the developing chick. Albumin, the egg white, holds water and protein. The more albumin in the egg, the more it needs to be turned. Precocial species like pheasants that hatch with downy feathers and ready to run, have less albumin and need less egg-turning than altricial bird species, which hatch completely dependent on their parents.

When
Ring-necked Pheasant are diurnal, active during the day and resting at night.

Migration
Permanent resident in Michigan. During the winter, flocks gather in cattail stands, grassy field edges, woodland edges and farm windbreaks to find safety from predators and blizzards. Leave rows of corn for pheasant winter food and cover.

Nesting
Ring-necked Pheasants nest in Michigan in April–May. Nest and chick predators include coyotes, fox, raccoons, skunks, birds of prey, dogs, cats and weasels.

Getting Around
Pheasants walk and run on their powerful legs. A pheasant hidden in the grass will fly almost straight up from the ground in quick, strong bursts. They are short-distance flyers. At night they roost in tree branches or nestle into stands of thick grass, cattails or cornstalks.

Where to Look
Open grasslands, prairies, agricultural fields, cattail marshes, shelterbelts, and brushy areas in the southern half of the LP. More common in the southern ⅔ of the state.

Year-round · Summer
Migration · Winter

Sandhill Crane

Grus canadensis

Height: 4 feet
Wingspan: 6–7 feet

Yellow eyes

Red patch on
crest of head

Long, stout bill

White cheek and
long gray neck

in flight

Males are larger than
females and their plumage
is similar.

Long black legs,
black feet

The long trachea
(windpipe) coils into the
sternum to produce a very
loud bugle call.

Do the Hokey-Pokey!

To a Sandhill Crane, it's all in the dance. A pair of cranes bonds to each other with a spring dance that rivals any hokey-pokey. "You leap up high, you spread your wings out wide, you put your bill up and you shake it all about. You do the Sandhill-Pokey, and you turn around your partner. Now you've done the spring crane dance!" They provide their own music with bugles and unison calls that can be heard two miles away. After the dance, the tune changes. Nesting begins and the pair brings as little attention to themselves as possible. The mud they spread on their feathers is not a spa treatment but acts as camouflage to blend into the brown grasses and sedges of their nesting area.

Habitat Café

Yumm.. bring an order of invertebrates, aquatic plant tubers (roots) and grains with side orders of small mammals and reptiles. Sandhill Cranes are omnivorous, eating both plant and animal matter.

SUMMER MENU:
 Plant tubers, invertebrates, some reptiles and grains

WINTER MENU:
 Weed seeds, field grains (corn)

Life Cycle

NEST Both the male and female build the nest in a wet area with cattails, sedges and other marsh grasses. While one is collecting plant material and tossing it over their shoulder onto a pile, the other is arranging it into a five-foot diameter nest. The inner nesting cup is lined with small, fine plant stems and twigs.

EGGS About 3 ½ inches long. Both the female and male incubate the 1-3 (usually 2) eggs for 29–30 days. Toward the end of incubation, parents may make a purr sound. Does this stimulate hatching or is it a response to hatching? It's a purr-fect mystery!

MOM! DAD! Precocial. The fluffy, yellow-brown chicks leave the nest within one day of hatching. By the second day, the chicks are battling it out to be number one. This aggression often results in the survival of only one chick. Chicks can fly at about 7 weeks of age.

JUVENILE The family stays together for the first 9–10 months, until about March. Groups of up to 20 young males migrate and feed together in a "bachelor flock." They look for a life-long mate generally after 4 years of age. Sandhill Cranes can live to be 25–30 years old!

Did You Know?

Night in the Museum? Here is one even better: Morning on the Marsh. America's first crane sanctuary, Baker Sanctuary, is open for public crane viewing on weekends in October. On the first October weekend, attend Crane Fest at the adjacent Kiwanis Youth Area (in Bellevue) to experience the sights and sounds of birds preparing for migration. There are more wildlife adventures waiting for you at Michigan's nature and environmental centers. See (pp. 196-197) for a listing. Explore!

When

Sandhill Cranes are diurnal. They are active during the day and rest at night.

Migration

Spring Arrival: mid Feb–March
Fall Departure: Oct.–Nov
Short distance migrant. Winter in large flocks in south Georgia and central Florida.

Nesting

Begin nesting in early April–May in Michigan's open marshes, bogs surrounded by shrubs and forests, and grasslands.

Getting Around

Sandhill Cranes have a distinct wing stroke pattern: quick and snappy on the upstroke and slow on the down stroke. Their neck is held out straight in flight. The main migration stopover is Jasper Pulaski-Fish and Wildlife Area in northwest Indiana.

Where to Look

Michigan's open grasslands and rural uncropped fields, prairies, and grassy roadsides. Beginning in August, visit these areas to view thousands of cranes staging for migration.
· Baker Sanctuary
· Haehnle Sanctuary
· Rose Lake Wildlife Area

Year-round   Summer
Migration   Winter

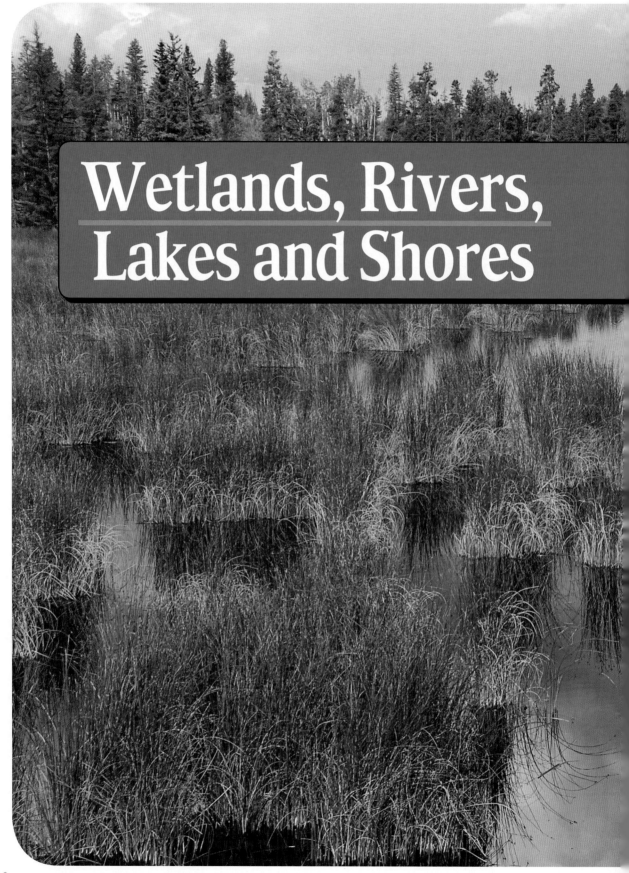

Wetlands, Rivers, Lakes and Shores

Water, water, everywhere! Michigan, land of the Great Lakes, has an abundance of wet habitats for birds. Bordered by Lake Superior, Lake Michigan, Lake Erie and Lake Huron, Michigan also hosts over 11,000 interior lakes, 36,000 miles of rivers and streams, prairie potholes, coastal and inland marshes, bogs, and more freshwater shoreline than any other state in the Nation.

143

Why Does Michigan Have So Much Water? Fire And Ice!

We can thank volcanoes and glaciers for Michigan's water. Lake Superior and Lake Michigan formed after ancient volcanic activity a billion years ago. The resulting lava flow was nearly five miles thick and caused the earth's surface to sink, leaving depressions (very big dents) in the land.

Bald Eagle

About 75,000 years ago, the Wisconsin Glacier—the last in a line of "glaciations" from the massive Laurentide Ice Sheet in Canada—moved into Michigan. During growth spurts, it sent lobes of ice deep into the state. The giant glacier spun its magic over most of Michigan, altering the landscape and leaving icy glacial meltwater that formed lakes, rivers and wetlands.

Its watery remains filled the sunken area as well, producing huge, deep lakes. Today, the Great Lakes are important to people and birds alike. They provide birds with major migration flyways. Travel the scenic roadways along Michigan's five major rivers and areas along the shores of the Great Lakes, for close-up views of migrating birds.

Wading Into Wetlands

Pull on your knee-high water boots and take a pal to an inland or coastal wetland, bog, river or lake. They are great places to find tadpoles, giant water bugs, dragonflies, crayfish, beavers, river otters and birds. Look for the unexpected, rare animals, too. Nearly half of threatened or endangered species live in or depend on wetlands.

Wetlands are important for other reasons, too. They help filter pollutants from farm field run-off, help recharge ground water supplies and reduce flooding by slowing the flow of rainwater on its way to streams and rivers.

Wetlands are also a great place to have fun. People canoe, hunt, fish, explore and enjoy nature here. Even though wetlands are very important places, many have been drained and filled to make way for houses, roads, stores

Great Egret

and farmland. Many of Michigan's original wetlands are gone. The good news is the DNR, conservation and sporting groups and private citizens are working hard to protect the remaining wetlands.

Wood Duck

Wetlands come in many shapes, types and sizes. We talk about peat bogs in the coniferous habitat section (page 26). Other wetlands are coastal wetlands, shorelines and beaches, shallow and deep marshes, wooded swamps, sedge meadows and river floodplains. Each kind of wetland has a special place in Michigan's ecosystems.

Where Do Wetland Birds Live?

Just as forests have different levels that support different species of birds, a shore, lake, wetland or river has different areas, or zones, that support various plants and animals that birds in turn use for shelter and food.

Perched on an overhanging branch, the Belted Kingfisher scans the clear, shallow water for small fish to spear. Spotted Sandpipers bee-bop along shorelines, while busy Sedge Wrens flit among the cattails and reeds. With legs nearly as tall as the marsh grasses they wade through, Great Blue Herons silently stalk small fish, crayfish, frogs and giant water beetles.

Belted Kingfisher

Dabbling in the shallow waters with tails tipped skyward are colorful waterfowl—Mallards and Blue-winged Teal.

Other water birds, such as Pied-billed Grebes, are diving for fish like mini submarines. In deep, clear waters, the black-and-white checkered Common Loon dives arrow-like into the water.

Watching from a throne high in a lakeside tree is the Osprey, ready to dive feet first and talons outstretched for a fish.

Some species, such as the Red-winged Blackbird, have adapted to living along Michigan's roadways where there are cattails to perch on and insects to eat. During May and June, take count of how many of the bold male Red-winged Blackbirds you see while traveling. Wildlife is everywhere!

Check Off the Wetlands Birds You See!

When you spot wetland birds, use these pages to check them off. The locations of these illustrations indicate where you might see them (air, water, edge or shore).

1. ☐ Sedge Wren (pg. 148)

1. ☐ Sedge Wren (pg. 148)
2. ☐ Common Yellowthroat (pg. 150)
3. ☐ Spotted Sandpiper (pg. 152)
4. ☐ Purple Martin (pg. 154)
5. ☐ Red-winged Blackbird (pg. 156)
6. ☐ Belted Kingfisher (pg. 158)
7. ☐ Pied-billed Grebe (pg. 160)
8. ☐ American Coot (pg. 162)
9. ☐ Blue-winged Teal (pg. 164)
10. ☐ Wood Duck (pg. 166)
11. ☐ Ring-billed Gull (pg. 168)
12. ☐ Mallard (pg. 170)
13. ☐ Osprey (pg. 172)
14. ☐ American Bittern (pg. 174)
15. ☐ Common Loon (pg. 176)
16. ☐ Canada Goose (pg. 178)
17. ☐ Bald Eagle (pg. 180)
18. ☐ Trumpeter Swan (pg. 182)
19. ☐ Great Egret (pg. 184)
20. ☐ Great Blue Heron (pg. 186)

Sedge Wren

Cistothorus platensis

Length: 4–4 ¹/₂ inches
Wingspan: 5 ¹/₂ inches

Long, slender and slightly curved bill to probe for insects

White striped crown and back

Throat and belly whitish

Females and males look similar

Short, rounded wings and tail are brown with black bands

Orange-brown rump

"See you at school soonnn!" The male sings this song of 3-4 notes and a trill.

Secret Agent Work Available

Zooming around in tall grasses and sedges like plump, brown dragonflies, these tiny birds are, come a little closer, *secretive*. Sedge Wrens operate in disguise, camouflaged. Like their woodland cousins the House Wrens, Sedge Wren males build 2–10 houses. Why build so many round basket nests in the sedges and reed stalks of Michigan's wet areas? It might be for decoy nests to fake out predators, or apartments for young birds when they leave the parents' nest. Or could it be to show off to the gals they are the big guy in the marsh? Solving the mystery of this crafty bird calls for a secret agent like you. Are those sunglasses with a detective camera in the rim? I hope they have a zoom lens!

Habitat Café

Yumm... bring an order of insects with side orders of spiders, ants, moths, caterpillars, crickets and grasshoppers. Sedge Wrens are insectivores. They search for their prey in moist soil at the bottom of sedges and grasses.

Today's Special
ladybird beetles

SPRING, SUMMER, FALL, WINTER MENU:
 Insects

Life Cycle

NEST The male builds the round nest in a thick stand of grass and sedges (grass-like plants with a triangle-shaped stem), 2-3 feet above the ground or water. He weaves dry and green grasses into a ball on the stems of live plants, leaving a secret entrance on the side. The female lines the hidden nest with fine grass, feathers and hair.

EGGS About ¾" inch long. The female incubates the clutch of 4-8 eggs (generally 7) for 12–16 days.

MOM! DAD! Altricial. Hatched blind and helpless, chicks depend on Mom to feed them small insects. Dad is busy building nests and singing in a new area to attract another female. If he does come to the nest, Mom may chase him away because he may destroy the eggs.

NESTLING As the chicks grow in size, so does the size of the insects they are fed. Mom is back and forth hunting and delivering dinner, back and forth, back and forth.

FLEDGLING Like little brown mice, the young leave the nest at about two weeks of age to move along the ground and hunt for food.

JUVENILE Young males invent most of their songs rather than copying the songs of other Sedge Wren males. Their general songs sing out, "I am a Sedge Wren."

Did You Know?

Male Sedge Wrens sing from a collection of 100 or more song types, sometimes even singing into the night. Why? With males competing for females, it's about setting up their home territory and getting a female to come over. When a female hears a male sing, it triggers body chemicals (hormones) that tell her body it is egg-laying time. To do this she first needs a mate— the male with the finest song in the area!

When

Sedge Wrens are diurnal. They are active during the day and rest at night. Males may sing into the night, serenading Sedge Wren females and evening visitors like you!

Migration

Spring Arrival: May
Fall Departure: Aug–Sept
Long-distance migrant by night to the southern United States and Mexico.

Nesting

Sedge Wrens begin nesting in May—June in Michigan.

Getting Around

Watch out underfoot! Sedge Wrens will run along the ground to escape capture from predators. By the time the predator arrives, the tiny bird is long gone! Their flight is short and quick with fast wing beats.

Where to Look

Wet meadows, prairies, grasslands and marshes with dense, tall sedges and grasses in Michigan.
· Seney National Wildlife Refuge
· Davidson Lakes–Ottawa NP
· Carlton Lake Wetland Nature Sanctuary
· Proud Lake, Detroit

| Year-round | Summer |
| Migration | Winter |

Common Yellowthroat

Geothlypis trichas

Length: 4–5 inches
Wingspan: 6–7 inches

Black mask with white upper band

Females do not wear a black mask and are more dull than males

Males have an olive green back, wings and tail

Bright yellow throat and upper chest

Common Yellowthroats are just one of Michigan's over 30 species of warblers

Immature Yellowthroats resemble an adult female

"Where-is-it, where-is-it" Males sing this song to say this is where my territory is. Then, if you are too close for comfort they call out, "Tchat!"

Masked Super Bird of the Wetlands

"Faster than a speeding bullet, able to leap tall buildings in a single bound"—probably not, but this black-masked super bird can down over 80 aphids in a mere minute! Nearly always on the move, Common Yellowthroats dodge detection in Michigan's damp areas of cattails, shrubs and grasses. You won't need x-ray vision to find them, just follow the sound and visual clues. Warblers warble—their song has a rhythmic move to it. Yellowthroats are warblers built for maneuvering through tight spaces. They glean insects in low plants with their short, thin bill. The latest marsh buzz? Clark Kent has something in common with this tiny super hero, but don't tell.

Habitat Café

Today's Special
leafhoppers

Yumm... bring an order of small insects with side orders of spiders and caterpillars. Common Yellowthroats are insectivores. A friend to plants, these warblers chow on leaf-eating insects. But watch out. Bigger birds like Loggerhead Shrikes will make a meal of Common Yellowthroats!

SPRING, SUMMER, FALL, WINTER MENU:
Mostly insects and spiders with a few seeds

Life Cycle

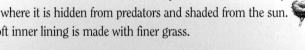

NEST The female builds the loose nest cup on or near the marshy ground where it is hidden from predators and shaded from the sun. The soft inner lining is made with finer grass.

EGGS About ¾ inch long. The female incubates the clutch of 3-5 eggs for 12 days.

MOM! DAD! Altricial. The orange-skinned, naked chicks are about one inch long and weigh less than a penny when they hatch—and that includes their black egg tooth.

NESTLING "Chac-chac-chac" coming from the nest means the chicks are begging for more food. Mom and Dad take different routes to and from the nest to detour any lurking predators.

FLEDGLING At only 10-12 days of age, the young leave the nest. Mom and Dad chip in groceries for a couple more weeks and then the juveniles are on their own.

JUVENILE By fall, young males begin to practice their beginning song before the family heads out on migration.

Birding Tip

Get a close up view of birds by using binoculars. (A pair with a large field of vision, 8 x 40 plus, works well.) First spot the bird without binoculars. Then, keep your eyes on the bird while you lift the binoculars to your eyes. Think of the binoculars as now being attached like a pair of eyeglasses and move them directly with your head. With practice you will be able to zoom in on quick-winged warblers! Tip: Spotting scopes in public wildlife viewing areas are free to use during your visits.

When
Diurnal. Common Yellowthroats are active during the day and rest at night.

Migration
Spring Arrival: April–May
Fall Departure: Aug –Sept
Long-distance migrant by night to wintering areas located along the Gulf and Atlantic Coasts of the SE United States and NE Mexico.

Nesting
Common Yellowthroats begin nesting in Michigan in May–June.

Getting Around
Common Yellowthroats hop and climb through thickets, grasses and sedges for spiders, insects and caterpillars. Their flight is flitting, short and direct. Flight Song: Males fly up with their tail bobbing and wings quivering to each note in their song. They come back down silently to land near their starting point.

Where to Look
Cattail, coastal and inland marshes, thickets, bogs, river edges, damp fields and shrub areas over all of Michigan. The southern LP is home to the highest numbers.
· Au Train Songbird Trail–UP
· Sandpoint Marsh–Pictured Rocks National Lakeshore

Year-round	Summer
Migration	Winter

Spotted Sandpiper

Actitis macularius

Length: 7–8 inches
Wingspan: 15 inches

winter

Females and males
look the same

White eye-ring

Black line from bill
across eye

Brown back

Long, thin orange bill
with black tip

White breast
and belly with
black spots

Orange-pink legs

"Peet-weet."
This soft call is made when
flying away from danger.

Teeter-Totter Shorebirds

Up and down, teeter-totter, Spotted Sandpipers bob their tail as they pick and glean insects, snail
and crayfish along Michigan's shorelines. The reason for the tail bobbing is a mystery. We d
know both chicks and adults bob their tails. At the least alarm, the motion may increase unt
the entire lower half of the bird's body is in a fast teeter-totter. With a little more alarm, the bir
may take to the air calling, peet-weet-weet. This action by Michigan's most common sandpipe
is repeated along shorelines all over the state in spring and summer. With a buddy, binoculars an
bird watching manners, explore bird playgrounds near you for teeter-tottering sandpipers!

Today's Special
grasshoppers

Habitat Café

Yumm . . . bring an order of aquatic (water) and land insects, tadpoles, small frogs, mollusks and crayfish. Spotted Sandpipers are omnivorous.

SPRING, SUMMER, FALL, WINTER MENU:
 Almost equal amounts of insects, amphibians and crustaceans

Life Cycle

NEST Both parents build the 5-inch diameter nest in a shallow 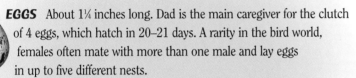 depression in the ground, hidden under grass or a small bush and lined with dry grass.

EGGS About 1¼ inches long. Dad is the main caregiver for the clutch of 4 eggs, which hatch in 20–21 days. A rarity in the bird world, females often mate with more than one male and lay eggs in up to five different nests.

MOM! DAD! Precocial. As soon as the chicks hatch, they walk to shore, usually with Dad—wee balls of bobbing fluff. They don't have tails at this point, just tiny rumps of fuzz. Their gray down is nearly invisible against pebbles and gravel. When in danger they flatten, becoming a part of the beach, or hurry to the water and dive for cover. One of the parents will spread its wings around the brood during the first week to keep the chicks warm and safe.

FLEDGLING Flight becomes routine when they are just weeks old.

JUVENILE At one year of age the birds are mature enough to date, mate and raise their own young.

Did You Know?

Spotted Sandpipers change their fashion each season. Just before fall migration, Spotted Sandpipers become unspotted. They molt, or lose their old feathers, and grow in new white feathers without spots. Their bill and legs turn to a dull yellow color during the winter. When it is time for spring and the nesting season to begin, they molt into spotted feathers again!

When

Spotted Sandpipers are diurnal. They feed during the day and rest at night.

Migration

Spring Arrival: April –May
Fall Departure: Sept–Oct
Short to long distance migrant. Solitary (alone) bird, even in migration. Migrates by night to wintering areas in southern U.S. and as far south as Bolivia and Brazil.

Nesting

Spotted Sandpipers nest in May–June in Michigan.

Getting Around

Spotted Sandpipers fly directly up from shore in a burst of take-off energy. In flight, their wings are stiff and flap only half-way up. This gives them a short, flickering style of flight. They dive straight into the water for safety and then straight out again from underneath the water!

Where to Look

Spotted Sandpipers live over most of Michigan along the shorelines of lakes, ponds, streams, rivers and wetlands.

Year-round   Summer
Migration   Winter

Purple Martin

Progne subis

Length: 8 inches
Wingspan: 18 inches

The short, wide beak opens large to catch insects while flying

colony nest box

female

Long, pointed wings of a swallow

Males are glossy blue-black all over

Females have a blue-black back and are gray and white below. They have a gray and brown collar at the back of their neck.

Juvenile looks like female with a gray forehead

"Cher, cher." Males and females may shake their body and flap their wings while giving this year-round call.

Forked tail

Waterside Condos

"Is anyone home?" Over one hundred years ago, Purple Martins made this call into lakeside woodpecker tree holes as they scouted for a place to nest. They weren't the only ones. House Sparrows and European Starlings, both bird species brought to the United States from Europe, were moving into the holes without even a courtesy knock at the door. They were replacing Purple Martins in their natural waterside woodland habitat. That is until people in Michigan began building. By 1900, Purple Martins were nesting almost entirely in colony nest boxes. Martins can be very sociable neighbors. When Purple Martins move into your Michigan neighborhood there will be fewer insects to pester you, so pass the hammer!

Habitat Café

Yumm . . . bring an order of crane flies, moths, butterflies, dragonflies and all other flying insects! Purple Martins are insectivores. When cold, wet weather lasts for more than 3–4 days and insects are not flying, Purple Martins can get very hungry indeed. If it lasts for too long, it can be dangerous for martins.

SPRING, SUMMER, FALL, WINTER MENU:
Entirely insects

Today's Special — horseflies!

Life Cycle

NEST The female builds the nest inside a nesting box, a gourd house, natural tree cavity, woodpecker hole or among rock piles. She uses weeds, straw, grasses and feathers. Mud may support the edges.

EGGS About ⅝ inch long. The female incubates the clutch of 4–6 eggs for 15–18 days.

MOM! DAD! Altricial. Both Mom and Dad feed the young and do diaper duty (remove fecal sacs).

NESTLING Feathers do not start to break through their thin skin until they are almost two weeks of age. When they do, they seem to grow overnight.

FLEDGLING At 4 weeks of age, flight feathers are complete. The young are coaxed out of the nest by their parents and led away from the nesting colony where they learn to catch insects on their own.

JUVENILE They group together in late summer and prepare for migration. On their spring return they are able to date, mate and raise their own young.

Unsolved Mystery

Before people began building apartment-style nest boxes, did martins nest together in colonies? Here are a few clues: Native Americans in Florida and North and South Carolina made nesting gourds for Purple Martins as early as 1712. In the northern U.S. there are records of Purple Martins nesting together among large lakeside rocks during the late 1800s. Send in your clues and mystery answers to the author of this book, www.adeleporter.com, for others to view.

When
Diurnal. Purple Martins are active during the day and rest at night.

Migration
Spring Arrival: April
Fall Departure: Aug–Sept
Short-distance migrant by night to wintering areas located along the Gulf and Atlantic Coasts of the southeast United States and northeast Mexico.

Nesting
Purple Martins begin to nest build in May and lay their eggs within the following two weeks.

Getting Around
Purple Martins are swift! They feed at heights of 15–45 feet. When chasing insect prey, they make sudden turns, speed, then spread their forked tail (brakes) and catch the insect. How do they take a bath and cool off? They skim the surface of the water and soak their belly feathers.

Where to Look
Shores of the Great Lakes and inland lakes in most of Michigan with the highest numbers found in the southeastern LP.
· St. Clair Flats & Harsen's Island
· Owashtanong Islands Sanctuary

Year-round	Summer
Migration	Winter

Red-winged Blackbird

Agelaius phoeniceus

Length: 7–9 inches
Wingspan: 13 inches

Males are glossy black

Females have a light eyebrow stripe. They are brown above with streaks of brown below.

Red shoulder patch with a yellow border

It takes young males two years to become black like Dad—called "delayed maturation"

"O-ka-leee!" means "Guys, stay away from my territory! But gals come on over—I have room for 3 or 4."

Safety in Numbers

Red-winged Blackbirds practice safety in numbers. (It's harder for predators to capture prey in a large group.) In late summer, redwings attend the annual family reunion with their cousins: starlings, grackles and cowbirds. Look for a flying river of blackbirds above the fields and across the sky at dawn and dusk in October and November. It can take more than 10 minutes for a massive flock of 10,000 birds to pass. Flocks feed in the fields during the day and roost at night. Female redwings migrate south in the fall before males. In the spring, males return first to Michigan's wetlands and roadsides to perch on a cattail, spread their red wing patches, and sing "O-ka-lee . . ."

Habitat Café

Yumm . . . bring an order of dragonflies, grasshoppers, spiders, beetles, moths and seeds like sunflowers. Their slender brown bill is designed to pick up insects and seeds. Red-winged Blackbirds are omnivorous.

Today's Special
snails

SPRING, SUMMER MENU:
 Mainly insects, some seeds and berries

FALL, WINTER MENU:
More seeds and berries, fewer insects than during spring and summer

Life Cycle

NEST The female builds the nest cup 3–10 feet above the ground in cattails, reeds and bushes over or near water. She weaves the leaves of water plants through the cattail stalks to make a nest cup. The inside of the nest is lined with soft, fine grasses.

EGGS About 1 inch long. The female incubates the 3–4 blue-green eggs with brown markings for 11 days.

MOM! DAD! Altricial. The female feeds the young and removes the fecal sacs (chick diapers) from the nest. If a predator comes too close to the nest, the female does a "flip-wing act" 5–10 feet from the nest.

NESTLING The chicks' eyes open when they are about one week old.

FLEDGLING Both parents feed the young for up to two weeks after they leave the nest.

JUVENILE Juveniles join a flock with other "teens." They feed during the day and roost at night. By fall they join a large group of both males and females and prepare to migrate to wintering areas.

Do the Math

Red-winged Blackbird chicks are fed insects. Insects are much higher in muscle and bone-building protein than seeds and berries. A male chick will increase in size by ten times in its first ten days. Multiply your birth weight by ten and you would be huge in only ten days. Do the math! But then, you don't need to grow into an adult your first year like a Red-winged Blackbird does. Answer on pages 194-195.

When
Red-winged Blackbirds are diurnal. They feed during the day and rest at night.

Migration
Spring Arrival: late Feb–March
Fall Departure: Oct–Nov
Short to long distance migrant. Red-winged Blackbirds gather in large groups of up to 100,000 birds before migrating to the southern U.S. and as far as Mexico and South America.

Nesting
Red-winged Blackbirds begin nesting in Michigan during May and June.

Getting Around
Look for Michigan's most common summer roadside bird sitting on top of signs, mile markers and fence posts. They walk on the ground to search for seeds and insects. Redwings fly in a pattern of closing their wings, dipping down, then rising again with a few wing beats.

Where to Look
Red-winged Blackbirds are found in all of Michigan; look for them in wet roadsides and fields, marshes and along the reedy edges of lakes.
· Super Adaptor

Year-round	Summer
Migration	Winter

Belted Kingfisher

Ceryle alcyon

Length: 11–14 inches
Wingspan: 20 inches

Head crest can stick straight up or stay closer to the head

female

Females wear a rusty-orange-colored belt

Juveniles look like adults but with a much smaller bill

Blue-gray above with a white throat collar and a blue band across the chest

Males do not have a belt

"Rattle, rattle, rattle . . ." This rattle call echoes against stream banks and riverbanks.

Expert Anglers

Scan the telephone wires and tree branches over a stream or river for the big-crested head and broad bill of this expert angler. Then sit quietly and watch as the blue-gray kingfisher studies the shallow, clear water for the movement of small fish, frogs and crayfish. Once it spots dinner, it dives like an arrow plunging its bill into the water. Captured! The prey is taken back to the perch where the kingfisher shakes its head and pounds the fish. This stuns the fish, breaking the bones of sticklebacks and bullheads, and the kingfisher turns the fish and swallows it headfirst. The kingfisher's two-part stomach is not equipped for scales and bones. Instead, these hard-to-digest items are formed into a pellet and coughed up.

Habitat Café

Yumm . . . bring an order of tadpoles, small fish, crayfish and dragonflies. Belted Kingfishers are carnivorous. They most often eat small fish that live in shallow water or stay near the surface. A kingfisher uses its thick pincher bill to catch prey. Look for its white wing patches in flight.

SPRING, SUMMER, FALL, WINTER MENU:

Fish, frogs, tadpoles and aquatic insects

Today's Special

leopard frogs

Life Cycle

NEST Both the male and female dig out a tunnel just a few feet from the top of a river or stream bank, a sand or gravel pit, or bluff. At the end of the 3- to 15-foot tunnel is a nesting room. The eggs are laid on fish bones and scales from spit-up food pellets that have fallen apart.

EGGS About 1¼ inches long. The female incubates the clutch of 6–7 eggs for 22–24 days. Dad sits in when Mom takes a break.

MOM! DAD! Altricial. Both parents bring a wad of regurgitated fish to feed the chicks during the first days.

NESTLING More like a cat in a litter box than a bird, nestlings back up and shoot their feces on the wall. They turn around and hammer soil from over the top of the wall with their bills.

FLEDGLING At four weeks of age, Mom or Dad sits on a nearby perch with a fish in its bill. When the chicks are hungry enough, they come out. Parents feed them less often as they grow.

JUVENILE Teens take ten days of fishing lessons. Their parents drop dead fish in the water and they capture it.

Unsolved Mystery

What kind of fish did the kingfisher eat for dinner last week? To solve this mystery, first find their perch and look underneath for pellets. Inside the pellets are the answers to their recent menu. You may find bones and scales that will help you identify the species of fish they ate. You can even tell how old the fish were by counting the rings on the scales! But be sure to wear gloves and be careful!

When

Kingfishers are diurnal. They feed during the day and rest at night.

Migration

Spring Arrival: March
Fall Departure: Sept–Oct
Short-to long-distance migrants far south as Central or South America. Some may overwinter in Michigan where open water remains.

Nesting

They begin to dig the nest burrow in April with incubation in May-June in Michigan.

Getting Around

Kingfishers perch on a branch, rock outcrop or on a wire over a river, stream or lake. Once they spot prey, they dive headfirst, catching it in their large bill. They also hover over an area for a short time to catch prey. Their short legs and feet with joined toes are not adapted for walking. They only need their feet for shuffling in and out of their burrow and perching.

Where to Look

Along Michigan's streams, rivers, ponds and lakes.
- Shiawasee National Wildlife Refuge
- Gogebic Ridge Hiking Trail
- Whitehouse Nature Center

Year-round	Summer
Migration	Winter

Pied-billed Grebe

Podilymbus podiceps

Length: 12–15 inches
Wingspan: 16 inches

winter

Square-ish, flat head

White eye-rings look like sunglasses with a fake nose

Dark brown all over with a white patch underneath

White bill with a black ring around the middle

Females and males look similar. Males are larger.

Flat, green, partially webbed (lobed) toes and feet

"Kuk-kuk-kuk-kuk-kuk-kuk-kuk, cow-cow-uh, cow-uh, cow-uh-cow-uh." Call begins soft and slow, but ends loud and fast.

Mini-submarines of the Marsh

Where did it go? Sinking in the water like a sneaky submarine, a Pied-billed Grebe can keep you waiting for its return. With their periscope eyes and camouflaged black and white bill the only parts above the water, they can stay hidden for a long time. The trick to sinking in the water at just the right level is the grebe's ability to force out and control the amount of air held in their feathers and body. Typical of diving birds, their legs are far back on their body and their wings are small. Don't let their small size fool you. They can sneak up on other birds in fierce attacks to claim their territory and protect their young. There it is—gone again!

Habitat Café

Yumm . . . bring an order of fish, dragonflies and nymphs, beetles, bugs, snails, mussels, frogs and crayfish. Their chicken-like, arched bill is just right for catching prey or crushing crustaceans. Pied-billed Grebes are both insectivores and carnivores.

SPRING, SUMMER, FALL, WINTER MENU:
Equal amounts of fish and insects, some crustaceans

Today's Special
feathers

Life Cycle

NEST As soon as the winter ice is melted, the female and male build their nest on a floating mat of decayed vegetation held to plant stalks in water at least one foot deep.

EGGS About 1¾ inches long. The female incubates the clutch of 4–8 eggs for just 23 days. She covers the eggs with a layer of plant leaves when she takes a break.

MOM! DAD! Precocial. Chicks can leave the nest for brief periods as soon as they are dry. They are in danger of drowning so they hitch a ride on the back of Mom and Dad. This cozy ride also protects them from predators. In only a few weeks, these little black-and-white striped "water skunks" can swim, dive and sink like their parents.

FLEDGLING The young grebes are able to fly and become independent when they are 8–9 weeks of age.

JUVENILE On their spring migration return, they are mature enough to date, mate and raise their own young.

Gross Factor

Grebes eat their own feathers throughout their lifetime, at times filling nearly half their stomach capacity. Parents feed feathers to their chicks soon after hatching. Biologists theorize that the feathers act to strain the stomach contents, preventing fish bones from passing into the intestines. Periodically, grebes spit up pellets of undigested feathers and other hard matter. Gross!

When

Pied-billed Grebes are diurnal. Normally, they are active during the day and rest at night. But during migration they are shy, nighttime fliers.

Migration

Spring Arrival: late Feb–April
Fall Departure: Sept–Nov
Short distance migrant wintering in the southern United States and northern Mexico.

Nesting

Pied-billed Grebes begin nesting in Michigan as soon as the winter ice is melted in late April and May.

Getting Around

Being wary birds, Pied-billed Grebes crash-dive into the water when they sense danger. This causes a spray of water several feet into the air, blocking the vision of the predator. By the time the spray is gone, so is the sneaky grebe!

Where to Look

Pied-billed Grebes are common summertime sights in wetlands, shallow lakes and ponds that have dense stands of cattails and open water.
· Nayanquing Point Wildlife Area
· Crosswinds Marsh, Detroit

Year-round   Summer
Migration   Winter

American Coot

Fulica americana

Length: 13–16 inches
Wingspan: 24 inches

diving

Females and males look alike

White forehead shield with bright red spot

Red eyes

Chicken-like white bill with black ring

Black all over

Stubby, upturned tail

Nickname: Mud Hen

Green-lobed toes and green legs

"Kuk-kuk-kuk!" means "This is my territory!"

Dare to be Different

Coots act like ducks. They are, however, in the rail bird family. Most rails spend their time wading along shores. Not the coot. It appears that they have adapted to being both a shorebird and a duck, or nearly so. Their body shape is flat, like a duck. Dense (thickly spaced) feathers on their underside are made for being in the water, like a duck. To get around on both land and water, their green feet are partly webbed, called lobed. Why the interesting chicken-like bill? It comes in handy for cracking open snails and other crustaceans. American Coots are a bit like the comical flip books that combine different body types to make a truly one-of-a-kind combination!

Habitat Café

Yumm . . . bring an order of aquatic insects, worms, tadpoles, snails and crayfish during breeding season. During non-breeding season bring an order of aquatic seeds, plant tubers and leaves. American Coots are omnivorous.

SPRING, SUMMER MENU:
 Plant matter, with equal amounts of insects and crustaceans on the side

FALL, WINTER MENU:
 Mostly plant matter, some insects and crustaceans

Today's Special
wild rice

Life Cycle

NEST The female builds the floating nest of plant leaves attached a few inches above the water to cattail and reed stalks. The nest is hidden in the edges of shallow lakes, ponds and wetlands.

EGGS About 2 inches long. Dad incubates the clutch of 6–12 eggs for 22–24 days. Mom pitches in at times.

MOM! DAD! Precocial. The black, downy chicks leave the nest soon after their down is dry. Frosted with white and wearing bright red patches on their head, the chicks could be in a Dr. Suess book!

Dad builds a brooding platform on a muskrat house, a mat of floating plants or a repaired nest. When the chicks are cold from the night air or storms, Dad or Mom keep them warm on the platform.

The chicks are fed insects during the first weeks by their parents. They feed themselves at 4–5 weeks of age. They add plants to their diet.

JUVENILE Juveniles leave the family group to join a flock of coots. When they are three months of age, they have grown to adult size.

Did You Know?

How many eyelids do birds have? Three. They have an upper and lower lid and a third, usually clear lid between the two lids and the cornea. The third lid is the nictitating membrane. This lid is used for blinking and keeps their eyes clean, moist and protected from their chicks while they feed them. In loons and other diving birds, the nictitating membrane has a clear center, which acts like a contact lens underwater.

When

America Coots are diurnal. They feed during the day and rest at night.

Migration

Spring Arrival: late Feb–May Fall Departure: Sept–mid Dec. Short to long distance migrant. In the fall, they fly by night to winter in the southern U.S., Mexico and at times, Central America.

Nesting

American Coots begin egg laying in late April–June in Michigan. They may have more than one brood per season.

Getting Around

Like many diving birds, the Coot's bones are solid and their legs are positioned far back on their body. Solid bones give them the extra weight they need to dive fast and deep. This helps them swim and dive, but makes for clumsy take-offs from the water.

Where to Look

American Coots live over much of Michigan in small bodies of water with reedy edges: marshes, ponds and reedy lakes. During October, look for coots on large rivers as they stage for migration.
· Wigwam Bay Wildlife Area

Year-round	Summer
Migration	Winter

Blue-winged Teal

Anas discors

Length: 14–16 inches
Wingspan: 23 inches

male

Look for blue wing patches and white wing bars

female

In flight, the top of wings are blue, white and green with a brown outer half

Males have a blue-gray head

A white, half-moon crescent between the bill and eye

White wing bars

Females are brown with a faint white patch at the base of their bill. No white band on forewing.

Orange legs and feet

"Quack" is a protection and defense call by the female during nesting season.

Dabblers

Is the duck stuck? No, the bird with its rump sticking up from the water is a dabbling duck. There are two groups of ducks: dabblers and divers. Dabbling ducks tip up as they reach down through the water with their bill and neck to forage for plant and animal food on the pond bottom. This is called dabbling. Just under the water, their feet paddle to keep them partly underwater. Blue-winged Teal and Mallards are dabblers. They live in shallow water. Diving ducks live in deep water and have small wings, square heads, legs located far back on their body and swim low in the water. Whether you are watching dabblers or divers, it is certain that you are dabbling in a super way to spend a day!

Habitat Café

Yumm . . . bring an order of insects, larvae and worms during the spring breeding season. In late summer through the winter months, it eats soft plant parts, wild rice, grasses, sedges and pondweeds. Blue-winged Teals are omnivorous.

SPRING & SUMMER MENU:
Mostly insects and larvae, some seeds

FALL & WINTER MENU:
Plants and seeds with some insects

Today's Special
tadpoles

Life Cycle

NEST The female weaves cattail leaves and dry grasses into a basket-like nest on dry ground near water. She lines the nest with her down feathers and arches nearby grasses over the top, making the nest nearly invisible.

EGGS About 1¾ inches long. The female incubates the clutch of 8–13 white eggs for 21–24 days.

MOM! DAD! Precocial. Soon after hatching, Mom leads the downy ducklings from the nest to water. They do not come back to the nest but for the first two weeks, Mom does brood them on chilly nights. The ducklings find insects on land and water on their own.

FLEDGLING Early nesters with an early fall migration departure, Blue-winged Teals mature very quickly. The young take flight at six weeks of age.

JUVENILE Mom goes her own way and the juveniles prepare for fall migration. When they return in the spring they are mature enough to date, mate and raise their own young.

Did You Know?

A migrating bird is busy with 4–5 major events in a year. Each event has to happen in order for the bird to survive. Between spring and fall flights, they have a breeding season and one or two molting periods. A female Blue-winged Teal must molt her feathers between the time she finishes her parenting duties and fall migration. Birds generally do not migrate with missing feathers. Males molt earlier and migrate south before females.

When

Blue-winged Teal are diurnal, active during the day and resting at night.

Migration

Spring Arrival: April–May
Fall Departure: Sept.–Oct.
Short to long distance migrant. Blue-winged Teals are among the first waterfowl to leave Michigan in the fall and the last to return in spring from wintering grounds in the southern United States through South America, including Brazil and central Chile. They fly in small flocks of 10–40 birds.

Nesting

Blue-winged Teal begin nesting in May in Michigan.

Getting Around

Blue-winged Teal take flight straight from the water! They fly at speeds of 30–50 miles per hour, and reach 60 mph during migration.

Where to Look

Watch for Blue-winged Teal in Michigan's shallow marshes, ponds and mud flats near land with a lot of short- and medium-height grasses that are used for nesting.
· Sturgeon River Slough NWR
· Muskegon State Game Area

| Year-round | Summer |
| Migration | Winter |

Wood Duck

Aix sponsa

Length: 17–19 inches
Wingspan: 30 inches

female

Female is brown. Breast white streaked above, gray below. White eye patch. White throat. Bushy, pointed crest.

Red eye and eye-ring

Iridescent green head and slicked back crest

Yellow and red bill with a black tip

Long, dark tail held at upright angle

White throat, chin collar and strap

"Jeeb!" is a whistle made by male Wood Ducks. Females call "Oo-eek, oo-eek" to their broods, and often give the call while in flight.

Another Michigan Success Story

Wood Ducks need habitat. They need trees with holes for nesting, food, shelter and nearby water. Drai̶ wetland habitat, harvest older woodland trees and hunt more ducks than can be raised each year an̶ Wood Ducks become rare. By the early 1900s, this was the case in Michigan. The good news? Wildlif̶ biologists studied the needs of Wood Ducks and came up with a plan. Nest boxes were built and place̶ near wetlands, lakes and rivers with the help of Michigan's sporting groups and individuals. Data wa̶ kept on the young that hatched. The number of Wood Ducks hunters were allowed to harvest each yea̶ was regulated. The plan worked. Today, Wood Ducks are all over the state. Success happens.

Habitat Café

Yumm . . . bring an order of seeds and tender shoots of aquatic (water) plants, fruit and nuts, insects and snails. Wood Ducks have a stretchy esophagus and store food. A researcher found one duck with 30 acorns in its esophagus! Wood Ducks are omnivorous.

Today's Special

acorns and dragonflies

SPRING, SUMMER, FALL MENU:

 Almost entirely plant matter, some animal matter

WINTER MENU:

 Mostly seeds and acorns, more animal matter than summer

Life Cycle

NEST The female makes the nest in a tree cavity or woodpecker hole, 6–30 feet above ground and near a wetland, a small lake or river. She lines the nest with her down feathers. Wood Ducks will also use a nest box lined with wood chips.

EGGS About 2 inches long. The female incubates the clutch of 10–15 eggs for 25–35 days. Sometimes, several females will all lay 30–40 eggs in just ONE nest box. One lucky hen will incubate all of the eggs!

MOM! DAD! Precocial. Hatched with eyes open, with warm brown and yellow down and sharp toenails. After a day of fluffing out, they climb to the edge of the nesting hole, pop out and float to the ground. Mom calls an O.K. signal, "kuk, kuk, kuk," and watches without helping. She leads her waddling puffballs to the nearest water. Mom keeps them warm at night for the first month. Young birds are able to fly and become independent at 7–10 weeks old.

JUVENILE Juveniles group in late summer to early fall. A female picks her mate on the southern wintering grounds. The chosen male follows her back to her original nesting area to make their new home.

Birding Tip

You can build a nesting box, too. Place the box in Wood Duck habitat, check it regularly and record nesting season data. The hens do not mind an occasional visit to peek inside. If you get up early on the day after hatching, you might be able to count the chicks that pop out of the nest and float to the ground!

When

Wood Ducks are diurnal. They feed during the day and rest at night.

Migration

Spring Arrival: late March–May
Fall Departure: Sept–Oct
Short-distance migrant to the southern United States and Mexico. A few hardy Wood Ducks overwinter in Michigan each year.

Nesting

Wood Ducks begin nesting in April–May in Michigan in natural tree cavities near water or nest boxes.

Getting Around

Wood Ducks fly straight and fast into their nesting hole—without bumping their head! They walk along the water's edge to feed. In the water, they are excellent swimmers. They dive to escape predators. Take-off from the water is quick and straight up with very fast wing beats.

Where to Look

Wooded habitat along rivers, streams and small lakes across all of Michigan.

· Shiawassee NWR
· Yankee Spring Rec. Area
· Maple River SGA
· Point Mouillee SGA

Year-round	Summer
Migration	Winter

Ring-billed Gull

Larus delawarensis

Length: 18–20 inches
Wingspan: 4 feet

winter

Yellow bill with
a black "ring"
near the tip

Gray wings

White body

Look for black
wing tips with
white spots

Yellow legs
and feet

Females and males
look the same

"Keeeeeaaaah—
kah, kah, kah,
kah, kah!"

Swashbuckling Pirates of the Air

Ahoy! The pirates of the bird world, Ring-billed Gulls pillage food treasures and fill their coffers with loot from ships that dump garbage overboard, as well as from landfills, parking lots, city parks, plowed fields, and along roads and beaches. They are opportunists, eating nearly anything: fish, rodents, small aquatic animals, insects, bird chicks and eggs, and even fruit and fast food leftovers. These swashbuckling gulls will steal fish right out of the bills of water birds like mergansers and snatch fish from the surface of the water. Living around ye lads and lassies of the land also provides ample treasure for pillaging. Use your spyglass to watch these flying pirates. Fair winds, me mateys!

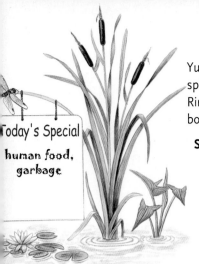

Habitat Café

Yumm . . . bring an order of fish, insects, spiders, earthworms and waste grains (corn). Ring-billed Gulls are omnivorous. They eat both plant and animal matter.

SPRING, SUMMER, FALL, WINTER MENU:
Animal and plant matter

Today's Special

human food, garbage

Life Cycle

NEST The nest is on a beach or island in the open ground on matted plants or in rocks. Champion recyclers, they may even line their nest with garbage.

EGGS Slightly more than 2¼ inches long. The female incubates the clutch of 2–3 eggs for 20–23 days.

MOM! DAD! Semi-precocial. Chicks blend into the shore with mottled brown, gray, or white down on their backs and white bellies. They can swim at 3–5 days of age. Lunch includes recycled food that their parents ate and then spit up near the nest. Scrumptious!

NESTLING With so many chicks and adults in a colony, how do they tell each other apart? Mom and Dad can pick out their chicks in a crowd of young by their unique facial markings. Chicks know their own parents' calls when they are 4–5 days of age.

FLEDGLING Young birds fledge when they are 3–5 weeks of age and leave the family group when they are able to fly.

JUVENILE The ring on their bill develops at one year of age and adult plumage (feather color and pattern) at three years of age.

Unsolved Mystery

Do birds play, or are all their actions related to survival? Watch gulls as they drop an object and swoop down to pick it up, drop the object and swoop to pick it up, drop the object . . . over and over. Are they in practice for catching prey, or playing a game for fun? Go ahead, play with this unsolved mystery!

When

Ring-billed Gulls are diurnal, active during the day and resting at night.

Migration

Spring Arrival: March–May
Fall Departure: August–November
Short-distance migrant to lakes, rivers, landfills, golf courses, fields and parks in the southern U.S. and northern Mexico. Ring-billed gulls are pushy when staking their claim to habitat. They are scavengers, eating anything edible. They do not depend on open water or specific foods and can come back north earlier than many other shorebirds.

Nesting

Ring-billed Gulls begin nesting in May–June in Michigan.

Getting Around

Ring-billed Gulls walk along shore in a side-to-side stride with attitude! Look for their wings held in a V-shape as they land on water. Floating atop the water like a buoy, they dip their head under for food. In the air, they are strong fliers and also hover and soar on thermals.

Where to Look

Ring-billed Gulls prefer islands, rock reefs and marshes.
· Coastal Saginaw Bay
· Kitchel-Lindquist
Dunes Preserve

Year-round   Summer
Migration   Winter

Mallard

Anas platyrhynchos

Length: 20–27 inches
Wingspan: 35 inches

female

Females, or hens, are streaked brown. Orange bill with small black spots. The speculum, a band of wing color, is metallic blue edged with white.

Male (drake) has a green head with a white neck ring and a red-brown chest

Male has a black tail curl

Orange, webbed feet paddle water and push the body down to reach plants

"Quack, quack" is made only by females. Males have two calls of their own, a nasal warning "rhaeb" and a short courtship whistle.

From Marshes to Malls—Mallards Are All Over Michigan!

Mallards are *Super Adaptors*! In cities, they have been seen nesting in downtown flower planters and balconies of buildings. Close to people or not, as long as there is shallow water and food near, Mallards are content. They eat everything from insects to frogs, plants that live under and on top of water, seeds from farm crops and wild plants. Watch for Mallards eating cracked corn under bird feeders. Mallards are also big eaters of mosquito larvae and pupae that live on the top of shallow water. With Mallards near, you can enjoy being outdoors with fewer mosquitoes to swat. Besides, Mallards smell better than insect repellent!

Today's Special
wild rice
and corn

Habitat Café

Yumm . . . bring an order of seeds and shoots of aquatic plants, grass, snails, worms and insects. Mallards are omnivorous. They eat both plant and animal matter, depending on the season.

SPRING BREEDING SEASON MENU:
Lots of insects and animal matter

SPRING, SUMMER, FALL MENU:
Includes aquatic plants and seeds

WINTER MENU:
Can include grains from farm crops

Life Cycle

NEST Built near water at the base of tall wetland plants or under a woody shrub. The female makes a few scrapes in the ground and lays her eggs. She then adds grass, reeds and leaves from nearby plants to make a nest rim around her body. Soft down feathers line the inside.

EGGS About 2¼ inches long. The female incubates the clutch of 9–13 eggs for 26–30 days.

MOM! DAD! Precocial. Mallard ducklings hatch covered with fluffy down and their eyes fully open. Mom is on her own with her large brood. The hatchlings are out of the nest after the first day and follow her to water.

Mallards dive for food during the first weeks after hatching, but this behavior all but disappears with the arrival of their flight feathers. Until they can fly at two months of age, they still need Mom's protection from snapping turtles, bass and raccoons.

JUVENILE At 10 weeks of age, young Mallards leave the family group to join a mixed flock of adults and juveniles. When they return in the spring, they are mature enough to raise their own family.

Did You Know?

While Mom is taking care of the ducklings, Dad joins a flock and stays very quiet. Male Mallards molt, or lose the old feathers and grow new ones, before fall migration. The bright breeding season feathers are replaced by dull camouflaged brown feathers called "eclipse plumage." During this time, they are unable to fly for a short period until the new feathers grow in.

When
Diurnal. They feed during the day and rest at night.

Migration
Spring Arrival: March–April
Fall Departure: Aug–Dec
Short distance migrant to the southern United States and Mexico. Some Mallards stay in Michigan during the winter, wherever they find suitable open water within a reasonable "commuting distance" of feeding areas.

Nesting
Mallards begin nesting in Michigan in late March–April.

Getting Around
Mallards are strong and direct fliers capable of reaching speeds up to 45–60 miles per hour. When they are alarmed they can spring straight up from the water. They use their wings and feet as brakes when making a landing into water! Mallards are also excellent swimmers.

Where to Look
Lakes, wetlands, rivers, parks and farm ponds. Explore city, county and state parks, and public areas or nature centers. Mallards may even eat cracked corn under bird feeders!
· *Super Adaptor*

Year-round   Summer
Migration   Winter

Osprey

Pandion haliaetus

Length: 21–23 inches
Wingspan: 59–71 inches

white crown
and forehead

dark line
through eye

long wings with
dark patch at
bend in wing

brown back and
upper wings

mostly white
breast and belly

Male and female
look similar,
females are larger

" Tiooop, tioooop, tiooop"
Males and females make this
whistle call when guarding
the nest.

Olympic-style Adaptations...

Ospreys dive in and escape with the prize—however wiggly and slippery it may be. They have Olympic-style adaptations for surviving along Michigan's waterways. Equipped with feathers so closely spaced and well oiled they are waterproof, they race into the clear water feet first to pluck their prize from the top few feet. Long and curved talons, barbed foot pads and reversible outer toes secure the desperate fish. If that isn't enough, two toes positioned forward and two backward lock the fish in a headfirst hold that makes for an aerodynamic getaway. Take to Michigan's waterways and cheer the performance of this wild champion.

Habitat Café

Yumm.. bring an order of fresh, wiggling, living fish, with a side order of fish. Ospreys are carnivorous. They dive feet first in shallow water for fish. Their catch is taken to a perch, often near the nest, where it is devoured with enthusiasm.

SPRING, SUMMER, FALL, WINTER MENU:

 Fish

Today's Special

fresh juicy fish

Life Cycle

NEST Ospreys build their nest on top of a tall living or dead tree or a cliff along lakes and streams. They have also adapted to nesting on nest poles placed close to water. The male brings in large sticks for the base and smaller sticks, grass and wetland materials for the inside. To keep the eggs from falling through cracks, the female adds flat objects last. Once a sturdy nest is built, the pair may reuse it year to year.

EGGS About 2 inches long. The female incubates the clutch of 1–4 eggs for 37 days.

MOM! DAD! Semiprecocial. The downy young beg loudly with the prize (food) going to the loudest. The third chick to hatch is generally smaller than the first chicks, making survival a challenge.

FLEDGLING At 7 weeks of age, the young exercise their wings at the nest rim and then leave the nest.

JUVENILE Ospreys do not leave their wintering areas until their second or third spring when they often return to the area where they were raised. They are mature enough at 3–5 years of age to nest.

Did You Know?

Ospreys are near the top of a lake food chain. In the 1950s, pesticides leaked into water supplies and were absorbed by fish that were in turn eaten by Osprey. The chemicals weakened the shells of their eggs and fewer chicks hatched. The Osprey population plummeted. With the banning of some pesticides, Ospreys made a comeback in Michigan, especially in the north. Currently the DNR is working to establish a stable population in southern Michigan. Lend a hand and report southern sightings to the DNR.

When
Ospreys are diurnal, active during the day and resting at night.

Migration
Spring Arrival: April
Fall Departure: late Aug–Sept
Migrate by day south of the U.S to Central and South America. Females migrate earlier in the fall and travel farther than males.

Nesting
The male Osprey arrives before the female to locate the nest. They begin nesting in April and May in Michigan.

Getting Around
Look for the dark patch at the bend of their long, narrow wings. Flight is steady and rowing with stiff wing-beats. They soar high on thermals to save energy. Ospreys don't wear nose plugs when diving, but they almost do. Their nasal valves close and prevent them from drowning when they dive into water.

Where to Look
Osprey fish in the clear, shallow waters along lakes, rivers and streams in Michigan's UP and the northern half of the LP. Ospreys are a state threatened species.
· Pigeon River Country SF
· Kensington Metropark

Year-round	Summer
Migration	Winter

American Bittern

Length: 23–27 inches
Wingspan: 3–4 feet

Yellow eyes on the side of their head

Long dark patch from eye down side of neck

Short, white neck with brown streaks that look like dry marsh grass

Compact, plump brown body

Adult females and males look the same. Males are a bit larger.

"Oon-ka-chuun-K!" means "Stay away, fellas—this is my space. Ladies, come over to my marsh-pad!"

Short, yellow-green legs and feet with very long toes

Onn-ka-chunn-K, oon-ka-chunn-K

Strange noises come from Michigan's marshes. "Oon-ka-chuun-K," it echoes. The deep thumps and ka-chunks of American Bitterns sound like a giant hobgoblin. Look in the marsh for a big blade of grass moving in the wind. Look closer. Stretching its white-and-brown neck to the sky, an American Bittern sways back and forth like pretend grass in the wind. The strange sound starts as the bird fills its esophagus like a balloon. Once the area is closed, this "balloon" shuts and it works like a drum. The sound from the syrinx bounces off the balloon-sac, making it louder. The bittern's body and neck stay blown out until the very end, making the last metallic note, "K," very loud.

Habitat Café

Yumm . . . bring an order of dragonflies, insects, crawfish, frogs, mice, small fish and lizards. American Bitterns are carnivorous. They eat only animal matter found around their marshy habitat.

Today's Special
small snakes

SPRING, SUMMER, FALL, WINTER MENU:

 Mostly insects, some amphibians, reptiles, mammals and crustaceans

Life Cycle

NEST The female builds a grassy nest on the ground or short mound hidden in the thick marsh plants.

EGGS About 2 inches long. The female incubates the clutch of 4–5 eggs for 24–28 days.

MOM! DAD! Altricial. Mom is the sole parent in this family, feeding and caring for the chicks.

NESTLING The downy, funny-looking chicks stay in the nest for the first two weeks, fed a liquid, regurgitated (spit-up) diet of partially digested fish, frogs, small snakes, insects and even mice.

FLEDGLING Young birds leave the nest after the first two weeks but hang out nearby for a few more weeks, begging extra meals from Mom.

JUVENILE Lacks the black neck patch of adults. When the teens return to Michigan in the spring from their southern wintering grounds, they are mature enough to mate and raise their own young.

Birding Tip

Covert (secret or undercover) hunting works well. The bittern wears its grass-like camouflage to hide it from the prey it is trying to catch. One of the best slow-motion actors on the marsh, a bittern moves from its "bill-to-the-sky-pretend-grass" position downward so slowly it is hard to see any movement. Its quick dart with its bill to grab prey is not slow, however. Once it catches prey, it shakes it and swallows it headfirst.

When

American Bitterns are diurnal, active during the day and resting at night. Some bitterns call into the night.

Migration

Spring Arrival: April–May
Fall Departure: Sept–Oct
Short-distance migrant moving from northern grasslands to wintering areas located along the Gulf and Atlantic Coasts of the SE US and NE Mexico.

Nesting

American Bitterns begin nesting May in Michigan.

Getting Around

Bitterns fly with their neck tucked in and legs hanging out behind. On land, they move in slow motion. Each leg is lifted slowly, as they spread their toes out wide before each foot touches the ground.

Where to Look

Tall, thick grasses and cattails of Michigan's marshes, lakes and ponds. The American Bittern is listed as a species of special concern in Michigan due to the loss and degradation of its habitat.

· Seney National WR
· Sturgeon River Slough WR
· St. Clair Flats &
  Harsen's Island

Year-round   Summer
Migration   Winter

Common Loon

Gavia immer

Length: 26–36 inches
Wingspan: 41–52 inches

Males and females molt summer feathers to gray winter plumage with white below

Red eyes filter light in deep water

Black head and neck

White-striped necklace

White breast. Black-and-white checkered back

Wailing means "I'm over here, fellow loons!" This can sound like the howl of a wolf or an eerie laugh.

Bird of the Wilderness

Common Loons spend almost their entire lives on water. With hundreds of lakes and plenty of fish, the Common Loon makes itself at home in northern Michigan. Built for deep lake diving, a loon flattens its feathers to push out air and become less buoyant. With its small, pointed wings to its sides, it plunges below the surface, paddling with webbed feet. In a short time, it strikes prey with its long, sharp bill partly open. (Loons will also stab intruders too close to their nest.) Parents train their young to catch prey by dropping fish in front of them. Chicks use their parents' backs as safety from predators and as diving platforms. How much fish does a loon family eat in a summer? Nearly one-half of a ton!

Habitat Café

Yumm . . . bring an order of fish (perch, lake trout, bullheads), minnows and aquatic insects. Common Loons are carnivorous. How do loons hold on to slippery fish? Their tongue and the roof of their mouth have sharp points that face backward like the barb on the end of a fishhook. A loon's throat expands for eating large fish.

SPRING, SUMMER, FALL, WINTER MENU:

🐟 Lots of fish, a few insects

Today's Special

frogs and crayfish

Life Cycle

NEST Loons will nest on a floating mat of plants attached to shoreline vegetation, close to the water on bare ground—even on a muskrat house. Parents add more plants to the two-foot diameter nest during incubation.

EGGS About 3½ inches long. Both the female and male incubate the clutch of 2 eggs for 28 days.

MOM! DAD! Precocial. The downy young can dive up to ten feet deep at only ten days old. Riding on the back of Mom or Dad protects them from predators such as Northern Pike, Muskies and Bald Eagles. The family moves farther away from motorboats and people to a nursery area, a quiet bay where the young birds have more protection from predators.

FLEDGLING Young do not fly until they are 12 weeks old. Both parents feed the chicks whole food for 2–3 months, even when the chicks can feed themselves at 6 weeks of age.

JUVENILE Juvenile loons migrate in flocks and may stay in wintering areas for their first two years. They are mature enough to date, mate and raise their own young when they are at least 4 years of age.

Birding Tip

Loons need large, deep lakes of 150–500 acres with space away from people and boats; they need about 200 yards of space (the length of two soccer fields). The loon makes a tremolo call when it is upset. Use a spotting scope, binoculars or the zoom lens on your camera to view loons. Be a Loon Ranger by staying clear of loon nests and reporting the location to Loonwatch, a program of the Michigan Loon Preservation Association, www.michiganloons.org/Loonwatch.htm.

When

Common Loons are diurnal, active during the day and resting at night.

Migration

Spring Arrival late March–April
Fall Departure Sept–Nov
Short to long distance migrant to Atlantic coast from N. Carolina to Florida and the Gulf of Mexico, just over 1,000 miles away. Flock on large lakes before migration. Juveniles leave 4–6 weeks after adults.

Nesting

Common Loons begin nesting in early May in Michigan.

Getting Around

Loons can dive 250 feet and stay underwater 5 minutes. Legs positioned far back on their body propel them in the water like a torpedo. They do not walk, but scoot on land and need a very large lake for a long water take-off.

Where to Look

Statewide on deep lakes of 150–200 acres with islands or shorelines with vegetation. Nesting is most common in UP and northern LP.
· Grass River Natural Area
· Tawas Point State Park
· Sylvania Recreation Area
· Seney National Wildlife Refuge

Year-round	Summer
Migration	Winter

Canada Goose

Branta canadensis

Length: 24–45 inches
Wingspan: 4–6 feet

in flight

gosling

Bill: Small saw-like points on the edges of the upper and lower mandibles help the goose grip plants and strip seeds from standing grasses

Look for their white underside and dark tail when they take off from land

Long, black neck with white throat patch

Females and males look similar, but the males are slightly larger

"Ha-roonk, ha-roonk!"

A Honking Success

Honk, honk, honk! A spring with few geese nesting? Around 1900, there were few goose calls. Canada Geese simply could not keep up with the draining of their wetland habitat, overhunting and poaching. They were nearly gone from Michigan as a nesting species when re-establishment began. Between the late 1920s–1964, the Michigan DNR released 2,500 geese at 30 Michigan sites. The efforts were a honking success. Surprisingly, this has led to some challenges for wildlife managers. Mated pairs of geese and their offspring come back to the same nesting place each year, causing populations to grow large in a few years. Wildlife managers work to balance both the needs of wildlife and people.

Habitat Café

Yumm . . . bring an order of roots, stems, leaves, fruits, berries and seeds. Canada Geese are herbivores. They also like to eat bluegrass—the kind of grass found on lake-shore lawns and golf courses.

Today's Special
field corn

SPRING, SUMMER, FALL MENU:

 Aquatic plants high in protein

WINTER MENU:

 Grass, agricultural crops, fruit, berries and seeds

Life Cycle

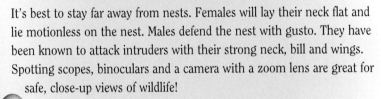

NEST Geese nest on muskrat houses, beaver lodges and floating mats of vegetation, or build their own nest. The female uses reeds, stems and leaves of water plants to make the bulky nest near water and lines it with her down feathers.

It's best to stay far away from nests. Females will lay their neck flat and lie motionless on the nest. Males defend the nest with gusto. They have been known to attack intruders with their strong neck, bill and wings. Spotting scopes, binoculars and a camera with a zoom lens are great for safe, close-up views of wildlife!

EGGS About 3½ inches long. The female incubates the clutch of 4–7 eggs for 28 days. Dad sits on the nest when Mom takes a break.

MOM! DAD! Precocial. The down-covered goslings are able to walk, swim, feed and dive just one day after hatching. Mom and Dad lead them to feeding areas. The goslings are fully fledged with strong flight feathers at 7–9 weeks of age.

JUVENILE Teens stay with their parents through the first year. They are mature enough at 2–5 years of age to date, mate and raise their own young.

Did You Know?

True waterfowl have toes connected by webbing to help them swim. The web is spread out to push the bird through in the water, then closed when the foot comes forward again. Geese and ducks have short tails that give them an advantage when it comes to speed, but not when it comes to making a sharp turn. Instead, they make use of their webbed feet to steer and brake.

When

Canada Geese are diurnal, active during the day and resting at night.

Migration

Spring Arrival: March–April
Fall Departure: Sept–Dec
Short distance migrant to central and southern U.S. Many over-winter in Michigan where they find open water.

Nesting

Canada Geese begin nesting in March–April in Michigan.

Getting Around

Canada Geese can move fast for large birds, flying at speeds of 40–60 mph. Their V-formation is energy efficient, too. Flying in the slipstream of the leader, the other geese face less wind resistance and use less energy. When the lead goose tires, it changes place with another goose. Now that's teamwork.

Where to Look

Canada Geese live in Michigan's open country with wetlands, ponds and lakeshores—even golf courses and city parks. Visit Allegan State Game Area in the fall to view thousands of geese preparing for migration.
· Kellogg Bird Sanctuary
· Chippewa National Forest
· Presque Isle Park

Year-round	Summer
Migration	Winter

Bald Eagle

Haliaeetus leucocephalus

Length: 31–37 inches
Wingspan: 7 feet

adult feeding juvenile

fishing

Large, yellow hooked beak for tearing apart prey

Dark brown-black with a white head

Females and males look the same. Females are often larger than males.

Large yellow legs and feet with curved talons for capturing and carrying prey

White tail

"Kwit kwit kwit kwit, kee-kee-kee-kee-ker!" This is fair warning to "Stay out of my territory!"

National Symbol of the USA

Michigan, with its many lakes and rivers, is home to an important breeding population of Bald Eagles. However, in the 1970s only 86 nesting pairs called the state home and there were only 800 in the lower 48 states in 1963. Thanks to regulation, the banning of the chemical DDT and restoration efforts, the Michigan population topped 450 pairs in 2006. To continue to nest successfully in Michigan, Bald Eagles need tall trees, open water within one mile of the nest, food, roosting areas and to not be disturbed. With more buildings placed near the water's edge, habitat is lost. You can be part of the Bald Eagle's success story by making choices that consider the needs of this fascinating wild bird of prey!

Habitat Café

Yumm . . . bring an order of fish caught at the water's surface, carrion (dead meat) and water birds including gulls and ducks. Bald Eagles are carnivorous. Eagles can eat large amounts of food and store it in their crop to digest over several days.

SPRING, SUMMER, FALL, WINTER MENU:

Mostly fish, some birds and a few mammals and reptiles

Today's Special
coots

Life Cycle

NEST Both parents build the nest, or eyrie, in the top of a large tree (cottonwood, red or white pine). The nest is a deep pile of large branches and sticks, lined with smaller twigs, grass, moss and weeds.

EGGS About 2¾ inches long. Both the female and male incubate the clutch of 2 eggs for 34–36 days.

MOM! DAD! Altricial. Covered with down for the first 5–6 weeks. Parents bring fresh food. The first chick to hatch is generally larger and may kill or starve the second, smaller chick.

NESTLING Feathers grow in at 5 weeks of age but young stay in the nest for 8–14 weeks. Before leaving the nest they practice flapping and landing skills. Half of all nest take-offs fall short, leaving the bird on the ground, vulnerable to predators. Mom and Dad come to the rescue and bring food until it can fly.

FLEDGLING Fledge at 3–4 months of age.

JUVENILE Juveniles gain their full adult plumage at five years of age. They stay with the same mate for life and remain in the same nesting territory each breeding season.

History Hangout

The National Emblem Law of 1940 made it illegal to kill any Bald Eagle in the lower 48 states. In Alaska, however, there was still a bounty of $2 for each pair of Bald Eagle feet until 1962, when this was outlawed. Today Bald Eagles are listed as a federal and state threatened species. They are also protected under the Migratory Bird Treaty Act.

When

Bald Eagles are diurnal, active during the day and resting at night.

Migration

Spring Arrival: March–April
Fall Departure: Sept–Nov
Short distance migrant. Some stay in Michigan all winter along open waters, while others migrate to states to the south.

Nesting

Bald Eagles begin egg-laying and incubation from late March to April mainly in Michigan's U.P. and northern L.P.

Getting Around

Bald Eagles use their powerful, broad wings to climb, soar and glide.

Where to Look

Bald Eagles can be found state-wide with the greatest numbers in the UP and northern LP in areas along lakes and rivers.
· Porcupine Mountain Wilderness SP
· Menominee River/Piers Gorge

Year-round   Summer
Migration   Winter

Trumpeter Swan

Cygnus buccinator

Height: 3½ feet
Wingspan: 5 feet

takeoff

Black bill

Males, called cobs, and females, called pens, are both white

The largest waterfowl in Michigan

Black legs and feet

Juveniles are gray for the first few years, reaching full adult white at four years of age

The windpipe (trachea) coils through the keel of the breastbone (sternum) to make a sound like the trumpet of a French horn.

Trumpeting Toward Success

Imagine finding webbed footprints the size of a party plate along a marsh! Trumpeter Swans left some of their last footprints in Michigan in the late 1800s. By 1935, only 69 individual Trumpeter Swans remained in the lower 48 states. It takes teamwork to bring a species back from the edge of extinction. In 1987, the local team of the Michigan DNR and the Kellogg Bird Sanctuary gathered swan eggs from Alaska to add to state swan restoration efforts. The teamwork has resulted in Trumpeter Swan numbers climbing to over 700 swans by 2005. You are part of the team, too, when you make choices that consider the environment and leave only a green footprint. That is something to trumpet about!

Habitat Café

Today's Special
wild celery

Yumm . . . bring an order of roots, seeds, leaves and tubers of plants that grow at the bottom and float on top of marshes and lakes. Cygnets (young swans) eat insects and snails for the first 2–5 weeks after they hatch, finding their meal by the color and movement of the prey. Adult Trumpeter Swans are herbivores.

SPRING, SUMMER, FALL, WINTER MENU:
Almost entirely plant matter, with a small amount of fish and invertebrates

Life Cycle

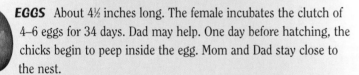

NEST The male and female build the nest on a muskrat or beaver house or dam, on a small island, a floating mat of plants, or they may build up enough plants to make their own nesting platform.

EGGS About 4½ inches long. The female incubates the clutch of 4–6 eggs for 34 days. Dad may help. One day before hatching, the chicks begin to peep inside the egg. Mom and Dad stay close to the nest.

MOM! DAD! Precocial. Cygnets can swim as soon as their down is dry, but they stay on the nest for a few days. They are brooded by their parents for the next three weeks until their new feathers grow in. Mom and Dad stir up snails and insects from the bottom of the marsh for the kids. Fast-growing cygnets need the extra protein found in insects and crustaceans.

JUVENILE Young swans stay with their parents through their first winter until they return in the spring to the breeding area. Teens hang out with their siblings until they are mature enough to mate and raise their own young at 4–6 years of age.

Did You Know?

The Michigan DNR Swan Restoration Program is funded by donations to the Michigan Nongame Fish and Wildlife Protection Fund. When you see a Trumpeter Swan in its habitat, it is a WILD reminder of how important each donation is in helping Michigan's wildlife. Spread the word!

When

Trumpeter Swans are diurnal, active during the day and resting at night.

Migration

Spring Arrival: April
Fall Departure: late Oct–Dec
Short distance migrant. Some overwinter in Michigan where they find food and open water.

Nesting

Trumpeter Swans begin nest building in late April–May in Michigan, often on muskrat houses.

Getting Around

Swans fly low over the water. They run on top of the water with their wings flapping to take off. Just after takeoff they pull their neck into an S and then straighten it out. They sleep with their head tucked under their wing.

Where to Look

Michigan's marshes and lakes.
· Kellogg Bird Sanctuary
· Lower Au Sable River Alcona Pond to Foote Dam Pond
· Allegan State Game Area
· Manistee National Forest, Manistee River

| Year-round | Summer |
| Migration | Winter |

Great Egret

Ardea alba

Length: 3–4 feet
Wingspan: 4 feet

Long, sharp yellow
bill designed for
spearing fish

Yellow eyes

During breeding
season the top of
the bill to just
below the eye is
apple green

A very long neck

All-white bird
with black legs
and feet

Females and males
look the same

aigrettes

in flight

"Frawnk" or, "Alarm!"
When you hear this call, take
the hint and move farther
away.

Great Egrets Escape Fashion Fad

Egrets wear beautiful, long white feathers (aigrettes) on their backs during their spring courtship
season. Women in the late 1800s to the early 1900s thought wearing aigrettes in their hats would be
just as gorgeous. Overhunting to pluck the fashionable feathers from the egrets nearly led to their
extinction. People took action just in time to protect egrets and other nongame birds worldwide with
the Migratory Bird Treaty Act of 1918. Great Egrets recovered and began nesting in Michigan again.
Trek to a river floodplain, wetland, stream, island and shallow shores in Michigan to watch Great
Egrets feathered for the spring fashion show.

Habitat Café

Yumm . . . bring an order of small fish, frogs, crayfish, dragonflies and whirligig beetles, tadpoles, snakes, lizards and small mammals. The long, sharp yellow bill is designed for spearing fish. Great Egrets are omnivorous.

SPRING, SUMMER, FALL, WINTER MENU:

Mostly fish, with some reptiles, amphibians and insects

oday's Special

giant water bugs

Life Cycle

NEST Both parents build the bulky, two-foot diameter nest of sticks and twigs in trees 10–30 feet above ground. Great Egrets nest on their own or in colonies with Great Blue Herons. Their feet have a special, long back toe to steady them while they perch in the nesting tree.

EGGS About 2 inches long. Both the male and female incubate the clutch of 3–4 eggs for 23–26 days.

MOM! DAD! Altricial. Both parents help feed the downy chicks.

NESTLING By the end of the first week, the chick's feathers begin to grow and are complete at 4–5 weeks of age. Like an umbrella, Mom or Dad stand over the young chicks to keep them dry when it rains!

FLEDGLING The young leave the nest to perch on nearby branches and exercise their wings at three weeks of age, but return to the nest for meals. The next week they dine out, and in yet another week or so they fly on their own.

JUVENILE Once they leave the nest, the teens go out to feeding areas during the day and return to the colony at night to roost.

Did You Know?

The Migratory Bird Act protects all migratory birds (and any part of the bird) wherever they spend their time. In addition, laws protect all wild birds in Michigan with the exception of the Rock Pigeon, European Starling and House Sparrow. You may not collect bird feathers, nests or eggs. You can keep the memory of what you find with a photograph, drawing or painting and by keeping notes in Journal Pages (pp. 189-191) for safe wildlife souvenirs.

When

Great Egrets are diurnal. They are active during the day and rest at night.

Migration

Spring Arrival: March–May
Fall Departure: late July –mid Nov
Short to long distance migrant, Central America. over-wintering in Alabama, Louisiana, Texas and south to Honduras.

Nesting

Begin nesting in May in Michigan.

Getting Around

Great Egrets move gracefully in flight with their neck tucked in an S shape and their black legs trailing behind! They will wade slowly during the day in water up to their belly, looking for small fish and crustaceans to eat.

Where to Look

Great Egrets can be seen near river floodplains, wetlands, streams and shores of shallow water with open vegetation. More common in Michigan's southern LP.

· Coastal Saginaw Bay
· Ludington State Park
· Harbor Island - Grand Haven
· Sutton's Bay Marsh

Year-round	Summer
Migration	Winter

Great Blue Heron

Ardea herodias

Length: 42–52 inches
Wingspan: 4–6 feet

in flight

Feather plume

Yellow bill

Adults have a white crown
and black areas on their
wing (shoulders)

Blue-gray with
a white throat
and head

Male and female
look alike

"Rok-rok"
means
"This is my space!"

Rok-Rok, Rookeries

Great Blue Herons nest throughout Michigan in colonies of often 100 or more birds, called rooker ies. Some heron rookeries are located along large rivers and forested islands. Going in or near heron colonies during nesting is not a good idea. You might cause the herons to abandon their young. Besides, a heron colony is a very smelly place. Many birds together can create a lot of droppings. Heron colonies are best enjoyed at a distance. Herons may fly out to feeding areas in wetlands over 30 miles from a colony. They are much easier to find and watch as they slowly stalk shoreline shal lows in search of fish and other prey.

Habitat Café

Yumm . . . bring an order of fish, frogs, crayfish, lizards, grasshoppers, mice and shrews. Herons grip or spear prey with their 6-inch pointed bill. Great Blue Herons are carnivorous. They eat only animal matter.

SPRING, SUMMER, FALL, WINTER MENU:
- Lots of fish, with fewer insects, reptiles and amphibians

Today's Special
snakes

Life Cycle

NEST Hundreds of Great Blue Herons nest together in the tops of tall trees in a colony called a rookery. The nest is built of large sticks. Herons will use the same rookery for many years. Some heron rookeries have been used for nearly 100 years!

EGGS About 2½ inches long. Both the female and male incubate the clutch of 4 eggs for 28 days.

MOM! DAD! Altricial. Both help feed the young.

NESTLING The chicks stay in the nest for about 7–8 weeks.

FLEDGLING They are about the same size as their parents when they leave the nest. The parents continue to feed them for 2–3 weeks.

JUVENILE The juveniles join with others their age, feeding and preparing for migration. They have a black crown, but it takes two years to grow a full feather plume. At three years they are mature enough to nest and raise young.

Gross Factor

Parents catch, eat and partially digest fish, frogs and other small animals, and deliver the baby food by spitting it up into the chick's open beak. As chicks grow, they take the food out of the parent's beak. Finally, the parents spit the food into the nest and the older chicks fight over the juiciest pieces. Chicks ward off threats from below by leaning over the nest and spitting half-digested fish on the intruder. Gross!

When
Great Blue Herons are diurnal, feeding during the day and resting at night.

Migration
Spring Arrival: March–May
Fall Departure: Sept. to Oct.
Short to long distance migrant to SE U.S. and as far south as Panama.

Nesting
Great Blue Heron begin to nest in April–May in Michigan.

Getting Around
Herons wade in shallow water, and sometimes stalk on dry land. Their toes spread out as they step on the ground, leaving tracks in the mud 6–8 inches long and 4–6 inches wide. Herons fly with slow, deep, steady wing beats, legs stretched out behind, and their neck bent into a tight S-shape.

Where to Look
Great Blue Herons can be found near rivers, streams, coastal and inland wetlands and lakes throughout Michigan with the highest numbers in the southern half of the state and the UP.
- Maple River State Game Area
- Alpena Wildlife Sanctuary
- Lake St. Clair
- Peninsula Point–UP
- West Bloomfield Woods

Year-round	Summer
Migration	Winter

YOU MIGHT INCLUDE:
• size, shape, field marks
• type of bill and feet
• shape of wings and tail
• feather color and pattern

Sample Journal Entry

Today I was looking in my binoculars and I saw a female Robin feeding her chicks. They were in my neighbor's tree on 5/13/08. The chicks were small and gray. They had bright yellow beaks. The female was brown with an orange belly, feet and beak. Her nest was made of sticks and twigs. She was very cool.

OTHER NOTES YOU MAY WANT TO INCLUDE:
• Date, time and habitat
• What the bird was doing (behavior)
• Song/call
• Alone, pair or group of birds
• Flight pattern
• Other signs like tracks, scat (droppings), nests, eggs, wood chips, wing marks in snow, ice crystals from a snow burrow

Glossary

Brainy Bird Words and Their Meanings

adaptation A physical feature, behavior or trait that a bird has developed to help it take full advantage of its habitat. American Robins are found all over Michigan because they have adapted to a variety of habitats for shelter, nesting and raising their young. They have also adapted to eating a variety of foods. A robin's diet includes worms, insects, seeds, berries and fruits. These meals can be found in rural, city or suburban habitats around the state.

altricial Baby birds that hatch from the egg helpless. They are naked, unable to see, walk, hop, fly or feed themselves, and need to be cared for by one or both parents.

anting Some birds, such as the Blue Jay, will place ants between their skin and their feathers with their beak. At times, some birds actually stand on an anthill and allow the ants to crawl up into their feathers!

binomial nomenclature A system of classifying and giving scientific names to plants and animals based on similar identifying characteristics. It is used to group birds together by which body characteristics they have in common. Scientific originate in Latin and Greek and remain the same all over the world. The scientific name for the American Robin is *Turdus migratorius*.

boreal migrant Birds that breed in Canada, but come south into Michigan during some years when their northern food supply is scarce.

bristle feathers Stiff, hair-like feathers made up of a firm central shaft (rachis). They usually grow near the eyes, nostrils and beak opening. Bristle feathers may protect the eyes from insects, dust and dirt, or help the bird funnel food into its mouth.

brood patch A bare spot on the chest or belly of a parent bird that is used to incubate eggs. The feathers in this area either fall off or are plucked out. Blood vessels next to the brood patch help keep the eggs warm. In most bird species, feathers regrow after the nesting season.

camouflage A bird's shape, or the color and pattern of its feathers (plumage), that helps it hide from predators or prey. The American Woodcock's plumage is similar in color and pattern to the brown leaves of the deciduous forest where it lives.

coniferous trees Trees that bear their seeds in a cone. Michigan's coniferous trees include red pine, white pine, jack pine, balsam fir, red cedar, white cedar, black spruce, white spruce and tamarack.

contour feathers These feathers overlap each other to give birds a streamlined body shape (a contour) for less friction. This helps birds fly faster through the air and dive faster in the water. Contour feathers are found on the body, wings and tail. They have a central shaft (rachis) with vanes on each side. Attached to the vanes are barbs. On each side of the barbs are small barbules that make a "zipper" to hold the feather barbs together. When the barbs unzip, the bird uses its beak to zip them back together while preening.

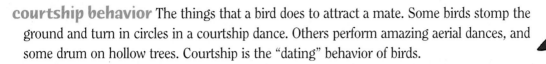

courtship behavior The things that a bird does to attract a mate. Some birds stomp the ground and turn in circles in a courtship dance. Others perform amazing aerial dances, and some drum on hollow trees. Courtship is the "dating" behavior of birds.

crepuscular Active during the twilight hours, which include the hours of dawn just before the sun rises, and dusk just after the sun sets. Crepuscular birds are active during the time between day and night when the faint light of sunrise and sunset provides them with protection from predators. American Woodcocks are mostly crepuscular.

deciduous forest A forest of trees that loses its all of their leaves each year. In Michigan, maples, oaks, elm, ash, fruit trees and cottonwoods are examples of deciduous trees.

diurnal Active during the daytime, or the hours that the sun is up. Diurnal birds feed, build their nests and preen during the day. American Robins are diurnal birds.

down feathers These feathers do not "zip" together like contour feathers, but stay fluffy. The air spaces hold the bird's body heat close like a warm blanket. Young birds often have down first to keep their small bodies warm until their contour and other body feathers grow in. Adult birds' down feathers are located under their contour feathers.

egg-tooth A newly hatched chick has an egg-tooth. This small, sharp projection on its upper mandible (bill) helps it to chip through the egg's shell during hatching. The egg-tooth is no longer needed after hatching and soon falls off.

field marks Each bird species has physical features that make it unique (one of a kind). These unique features can help you to identify it. Field marks include feather color, feather pattern, a bird's basic body shape and size. Other field marks include the shape and size of the bird's bill, feet, wings and tail. An eye-ring (which gives the bird the appearance of wearing a pair of glasses) or a crest on the top of its head are also field marks.

fledgling Young birds that have just learned to fly on their own and have left the family nest are called fledglings. To fledge is to be fully feathered and be able to sustain flight.

filoplume feather Delicate, hair-like feathers that help a bird adjust the position of its contour feathers for better flight. Filoplume feathers are scattered over a bird's body. They are sensitive enough to move with the slightest breeze, and send information to nerve cells at their bases.

foraging Gathering food.

game wildlife Birds and other wildlife that can be legally hunted under Michigan law during designated times of the year. Hunting seasons and limits are specific to each species.

glean To collect or pick up, often referring to gathering food. When a bird picks insect larvae from cracks in tree bark, or spilled grain from a harvested farm field, it is said to be "gleaning."

habitat The place where a bird lives. For a Mallard, home is a shallow lake or wetland habitat where it can reach for the plants and animals on the lake or wetland bottom with its long neck and bill. For a Pileated Woodpecker, home is in a forest habitat with trees big enough for it to make large nesting and roosting holes.

hawking The act of catching insects on the wing in short, quick flights.

juvenile A young bird that has grown to be independent of its parents (it can fly and find food, water and shelter on its own) but is not yet mature enough to breed. Many smaller birds pass through this stage in their first year; larger birds can remain a juvenile for four or five years. They are the adolescents and teenagers of the bird world.

lift This is what allows a bird to defy gravity and get off the ground. Lift is made by the force of the air pressure underneath the wings, which is greater than the air pressure above the wings, and results in a raising force. The shape of a bird's wings is what makes this work. The top side of the wing is convex (curved), and the bottom is flatter. The air rushing past the wing is divided in two flows: one over the top of the wing and the other past the bottom of the wing. The top air moves faster. This causes the air beneath the wing to go slower and increases the air pressure under the wing—the bird is lifted off the ground. The Swiss scientist **Daniel Bernoulli** (1700–1782) discovered this principle of flight, which is now called **Bernoulli's Principle**.

migration The seasonal movement of birds or animals from one region to another. Purple Martins migrate to wintering grounds in South America in early September and return to Michigan the following spring to nest and raise their young.

molt When a bird sheds its old feathers and grows in new ones to replace them.

navigation How a bird finds its way, such as during migration.

neotropical migrant A bird that breeds in Michigan, but migrates to wintering areas in Central and South America. Includes both mid-distance Central American and long-distance South American migrants.

nocturnal Active during the night. Birds that are nocturnal are active feeding, nest building and preening during the night. Great Horned Owls are nocturnal birds.

nongame wildlife Birds and animals protected by state or national laws from trapping and hunting. Most birds in this book are nongame birds. There is no designated time or "season" to legally hunt them. Game birds, however, can be legally hunted.

ornithology The study of birds. The segment "ology" in a word means the study of, and "ornith" is associated with birds. An ornithologist is a scientist who studies birds.

overwinter To spend the winter. Many Canada Geese overwinter in Michigan.

permanent resident Birds that breed and remain in Michigan all year. Black-capped Chickadees and Blue Jays are permanent residents in Michigan.

phenology The study of the changing seasons.

plumage A bird's plumage refers to all of its feathers together.

prairie Land covered with native grasses and flowering plants with few to no trees. In Michigan, parts of the state were once covered by prairie, described by Native Americans and pioneers alike as an ocean of grass. Today, only small remnants of the original prairie remain in publicly and privately owned areas. Plants and animals that have adapted over tens of thousands of years to the conditions of the prairie habitat can be found on these unique areas of Michigan.

precocial Chicks that hatch able to see, walk, hop or fly and feed themselves. They need only limited care by one or both parents. The role of the parents in precocial birds is usually to lead the young to food, offer protection from predators, and provide brooding in weather and temperature extremes. The young of many ground-nesting birds such as the Killdeer and Canada Goose are precocial.

predator A bird or animal that captures other living creatures to eat. A Cooper's Hawk is a predator of small mammals that it catches for lunch.

preening When a bird arranges, cleans, fluffs and straightens its feathers.

prey A bird or animal that is captured and eaten by a predator. The small mammals captured for lunch by a Cooper's Hawk are considered its prey.

semiplume feather A combination of a contour feather and a down feather. It has a stiff shaft and soft down vanes that serve as extra insulation to keep a bird warm.

short distance migrant A bird that breeds in Michigan but winters just far enough south to avoid extreme temperatures and snowfall.

super adaptor A bird that is able to live in a variety of habitats.

syrinx The vocal organ of a bird similar to the larynx (voice box) in humans. Birds use the syrinx to call and sing (page 92).

territory A bird's territory is the space that it defends from other birds (and sometimes mammals such as squirrels) for feeding, courtship, nesting and raising its young.

undulating To move in waves, in an up-and-down way.

uropygium gland A gland located above a bird's tail that holds oil. The bird squeezes the gland with its bill to get the oil and then spreads the oil onto its feathers for conditioning.

warm-blooded All birds are warm-blooded. They can keep a constant body temperature no matter how hot or cold the weather. Mammals like you are also warm-blooded. Reptiles and amphibians are cold-blooded. They take on the temperature of their surroundings.

webbed feet When a bird's toes are connected to one another by thick skin, the bird is said to have webbed feet. Mallards, Canada Geese and Blue-winged Teals have webbed feet that help them paddle through the water.

wetlands Areas of land that hold water in their soils or are covered with water during all or part of the year. Wetlands can be found separate from other bodies of water, or associated with the shallow edges of a river or lake. Bogs are a special kind of wetland that are very acidic and have a buildup of peat. Plants and animals living in wetland habitats have special adaptations to make the most of the watery conditions.

Do the Math Answer Key

Do the math on your own first and then check if the answer is figured correctly. If you have not, review the equations in this answer key to find where you worked the math differently. Use your brain power, you can do it!

Ruby-throated Hummingbird (pg. 30)

This solution is based on the weight of a 100 pound person. Put your weight in and rework the problem.

Step #1:   Change the percent to a decimal

$$30\% = 30. = .30$$

Step #2:   .30 X 100 pounds of body weight = 30 pounds increase in body weight

Ruffed Grouse (pg. 54)

-27° at the snow's surface + 24° seven inches under the snow = 51 degrees of difference between the temperature at the surface of the snow and the temperature seven inches under the snow. Wow, snow is an efficient insulator.

Great Gray Owl (pg. 58)

Ask a Michigan DNR wildlife biologist for the year of the last great gray owl invasions. Mark each invasion with an X above the year on the chart below. When might the next one be? Over time, a pattern may form. Do the Math!

2016	2017	2018	2019	2020	2021	2022	2023	2024	2025	2026

American Robin (pg. 88)

14 feet of earthworms per day x 7 days = A robin can eat 98 feet of earthworms in one week! Line up 98 feet of gummy worms, pipe cleaners or string on your sidewalk or driveway to see this amazing feat for yourself.

Cooper's Hawk (pg. 100)

66 prey X 3 chicks = 198 prey needed to feed 3 young hawks for six weeks

66 prey X 4 chicks = 264 prey needed to feed 4 young hawks for six weeks

66 prey X 5 chicks = 330 prey needed to feed 5 young hawks for six weeks

Pileated Woodpecker (pg. 102)

15 drumbeats in one second X 60 seconds = 900 drumbeats in one minute

900 drumbeats in one minute X 10 minutes = 9000 drumbeats in ten minutes

Red-winged Blackbird (pg. 156)

This solution is based on a birth weight of 8 pounds. Place your birth weight in and rework the problem.

8 pounds birth weight x 10 = A weight gain of 80 pounds in just 10 days.

Use the Space Below to Work the Numbers

Great Places to Learn More About Birds

Share this chart and map with your family and friends to find places near you to visit and learn more about Michigan's amazing birds and the habitats they live in.

Map #	Center Name	City	Phone Number	Web or Email Address
1	Blandford Nature Center	Grand Rapids	616-735-6240	blandfordnaturecenter.org
2	Boardman River Nature Center	Traverse City	231-941-0960	natureiscalling.org/explore/nature-center/
3	Burgess-Shadbush Nature Center	Shelby Township	586-323-2478	www.shelbytwp.org/departments/prm/burgess-shadbush_nature_center/index.html
4	Chippewa Nature Center	Midland	989-631-0830	www.chippewanaturecenter.org
5	Howard Christensen Nature Center	Kent City	616-675-3158	www.howardchristensen.org
6	Dahlem Environmental Education Center	Jackson	517-782-3453	www.dahlemcenter.org/
7	DeGraaf Nature Center	Holland	616-355-1057	www.cityofholland.com/degraafnaturecenter
8	Dinosaur Hill Nature Preserve	Rochester	248-656-0999	www.dinosaurhill.org
9	Drayton Plains Nature Center	Waterford Township	248-674-2119	www.waterfordmi.gov/Facilities/Facility/Details/Drayton-Plains-Nature-Center-1
10	Ebersole Environmental Education Center	Wayland	517-755-5000 or 269-792-6294	ebersole.lansingschools.net
11	Fenner Nature Center	Lansing	517-483-4224	mynaturecenter.org
12	Fernwood Botanical Garden & Nature Preserve	Niles	269-695-6491	www.fernwoodbotanical.org/
13	For-Mar Nature Preserve & Arboretum	Burton	810-736-7100	geneseecountyparks.org/explore/for-mar-nature-preserve-and-arboretum-and-forbes-martha-merkley-visitor-center/
14	Fowler Center for Outdoor Learning	Mayville	989-673-2050	thefowlercenter.org
15	The Nature Center at Friendship Woods	Madison Heights	248-585-0100	www.madison-heights.org
16	Gillette Sand Dune Visitor Center at P. J. Hoffmaster State Park	Muskegon	231-798-3573	www.michigan.gov/dnr/0,4570,7-350-79133_79207_81177---,00.html
17	Green Point Environmental Learning Center	Saginaw	989-759-1669	www.fws.gov/refuge/Shiawassee/
18	Harris Nature Center	Okemos	517-349-3866	www.meridian.mi.us/visitors/hidden-gems/visit-harris-nature-center
19	Hartley Outdoor Education Center	St. Charles	989-865-6295	www.sisd.cc/District/Department/19-Hartley-Outdoor-Education-Center
20	E. Dale Fisk Hawk Woods Nature Center	Auburn Hills	248-370-9353	auburnhills.org/departments/parks_and_recreation/parks_and_facilities/hawk_woods_nature_center.php
21	Howell Nature Center	Howell	517-546-0249	howellnaturecenter.org
22	Huron County Nature Center	Port Austin	989-551-8400	www.huronnaturecenter.org/
23	Indian Springs Environmental Discovery Center	White Lake	248-625-7280	www.metroparks.com/facilities-education/indian-springs-environmental-discovery-center/
24	E. L. Johnson Nature Center	Bloomfield Hills	248-341-6485	www.bloomfield.org/schools/el-johnson-nature-center
25	Carl T. Johnson Hunting & Fishing Center	Cadillac	231-779-1321	www.michigan.gov/huntfishcenter
26	Kalamazoo Nature Center	Kalamazoo	269-381-1574	naturecenter.org
27	Kensington Nature Center	Milford	810-227-8917	www.metroparks.com/facilities-education/kensington-nature-center/
28	Lake St. Clair Nature Center	Harrison Township	586-463-4332	www.metroparks.com/facilities-education/lake-st-clair-metropark-nature-center/
29	Leslie Science and Nature Center	Ann Arbor	734-997-1553	www.lesliesnc.org
30	Lewis E. Wint Nature Center	Clarkston	248-625-6473	www.oakgov.com/parks/parksandtrails/Independence-Oaks/Pages/Wint-Nature-Center.aspx
31	Love Creek Nature Center	Berrien Center	269-471-2617	berriencounty.org/1299/Love-Creek-County-Park
32	MooseWood Nature Center	Marquette	906-228-6250	moosewood.org

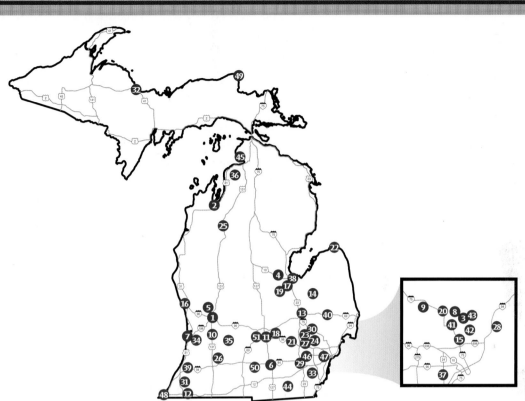

Map #	Center Name	City	Phone Number	Web Address
33	Oakwoods Nature Center	Belleville	734-782-3956	www.metroparks.com/facilities-education/oakwoods-metropark-nature-center/
34	Outdoor Discovery Center	Holland	616-393-9453	outdoordiscovery.org
35	Pierce Cedar Creek Institute	Hastings	269-721-4190	www.cedarcreekinstitute.org
36	Raven Hill Discovery Center	East Jordan	231-536-3369	miravenhill.org
37	Rouge River Bird Observatory	Dearborn	313-593-5338	www.rrbo.org
38	Saginaw Bay Visitors Center	Bay City	989-667-0717	www.michigan.gov/dnr/0,4570,7-350-79133_79207_81181---,00.html
39	Sarett Nature Center	Benton Harbor	269-927-4832	sarett.com
40	Seven Ponds Nature Center	Dryden	810-796-3200	www.sevenponds.org
41	Stage Nature Center	Troy	248-688-9703	troynaturesociety.org
42	Sterling Heights Nature Center	Sterling Heights	586-446-2710	www.sterling-heights.net/302/Nature-Center
43	Stony Creek Nature Center	Shelby Township	586-781-9113	www.metroparks.com/facilities-education/stony-creek-metropark-nature-center/
44	Stubnitz Environmental Education Center	Adrian	517-265-6691	www.lisd.us/seec/
45	Thorne Swift Nature Preserve	Harbor Springs	231-526-6401	landtrust.org/thorne-swift-nature-preserve/
46	Thurston Nature Center	Ann Arbor	734-994-1970	thurstonnaturecenter.org/
47	University of Michigan-Dearborn Environmental Interpretive Center	Dearborn	313-593-5338	umdearborn.edu/eic/
48	Warren Woods Nature Study Area	Three Oaks	269-426-4013	www.michigan.gov/dnr/0,4570,7-350-79133_79200_31427-54041--,00.html
49	Whitefish Point Bird Observatory	Paradise	see website	www.wpbo.org
50	Whitehouse Nature Center	Albion	517-629-0582	www.albion.edu/about-albion/whitehouse-nature-center
51	Woldumar Nature Center	Lansing	517-322-0030	www.woldumar.org/

Bird Species by Taxonomic Order

This taxonomic list draws from the common Linnean system, which classifies birds and other living things by their morphological (physical) features. It was developed over two hundred years ago by Carl Linnaeus, a Swedish naturalist. Learn more about scientific names on page 13, in "Binomial Nomenclature."

ANSERIFORMES: DUCKS, GEESE, SWANS, WATERFOWL
Canada Goose
Trumpeter Swan
Wood Duck
Mallard
Blue-winged Teal

GALLIFORMES: CHICKENS, QUAIL, TURKEYS, PHEASANTS
Ring-necked Pheasant
Ruffed Grouse
Sharp-tailed Grouse
Wild Turkey

GAVIIFORMES: LOONS
Common Loon

PODICIPEDIFORMES: GREBES
Pied-billed Grebe

CICONIIFORMES: HERONS, BITTERNS, EGRETS
American Bittern
Great Blue Heron
Great Egret

FALCONIFORMES: EAGLES, HAWKS, FALCONS
Osprey
Bald Eagle
Northern Harrier
Cooper's Hawk
Red-tailed Hawk
American Kestrel

GRUIFORMES: CRANES, COOTS, RAILS
American Coot
Sandhill Crane

CHARADRIIFORMES: SHOREBIRDS, GULLS, TERNS, PLOVERS, SANDPIPERS
Killdeer
Spotted Sandpiper
American Woodcock
Ring-billed Gull

COLUMBIFORMES: DOVES, PIGEONS
Mourning Dove

STRIGIFORMES: OWLS
Eastern Screech-Owl
Great Horned Owl
Snowy Owl
Barred Owl
Great Gray Owl

APODIFORMES: HUMMINGBIRDS
Ruby-throated Hummingbird

CORACIIFORMES: KINGFISHERS
Belted Kingfisher

PICIFORMES: WOODPECKERS
Yellow-bellied Sapsucker
Downy Woodpecker
Northern Flicker
Pileated Woodpecker

PASSERIFORMES: PERCHING BIRDS, SONGBIRDS
Eastern Kingbird
Gray Jay
Blue Jay
Common Raven
Horned Lark
Purple Martin
Black-capped Chickadee
Boreal Chickadee

Red-breasted Nuthatch
White-breasted Nuthatch
Brown Creeper
House Wren
Sedge Wren
Golden-crowned Kinglet
Eastern Bluebird
American Robin
Brown Thrasher
Ovenbird
Common Yellowthroat
Savannah Sparrow
White-throated Sparrow
Dark-eyed Junco
Northern Cardinal
Rose-breasted Grosbeak
Indigo Bunting
Bobolink
Red-winged Blackbird
Eastern Meadowlark
Baltimore Oriole
Purple Finch
American Goldfinch
Evening Grosbeak

This order follows the most recent version accepted by the American Ornithologists' Union, recently revised to include DNA evidence.

References

The resources used to prepare this book include numerous reports and surveys, many from the Michigan Department of Natural Resources. A complete reference list can be found at Adele Porter's author website: www.adeleporter.com. General references and sources of additional information include the following books, reports and publications:

Albert, D.A. *Between Land and Lake: Michigan's Great Lakes Coastal Wetlands*. Michigan Natural Features Inventory, Bulletin E-2902. East Lansing: Michigan State University Extension, 2003.

Brewer, R., G.A. McPeeke, R.J. Adams. *Atlas of Breeding Birds of Michigan*. Michigan State University Press, 1991.

Chartier, A.T., J. Ziarno. *Birder's Guide to Michigan*. Colorado Springs: American Birding Association, 2004.

Dechant, J.A., et al., *Effects of management practices on grassland birds: Bobolink, Grasshopper Sparrow, Greater Prairie-Chicken, Horned Lark, Northern Harrier, Eastern Meadowlark*. Jamestown: Northern Prairie Wildlife Research Center, 1999 (revised 2002).

Dickman, D., L.A. Leefers. *The Forests of Michigan*. Ann Arbor: University of Michigan Press, 2003.

Eagle, A.C., E.M. Hay-Chmielewski, K.T. Cleveland, A.L. Derosier, M.E. Herbert, and R.A. Rustem, eds. *Michigan's Wildlife Action Plan*. Lansing: Michigan Department of Natural Resources, 2005. http://www.michigan.gov/dnrwildlifeactionplan

Gill, F., and A. Poole, eds. *The Birds of North America, volumes 1–18*. Philadelphia: Academy of Natural Sciences; Washington, D.C.: American Ornithologists' Union; Ithaca: Cornell Lab of Ornithology, 2002.

Kost, M.A., et al. *Natural Communities of Michigan: Classification and Description*. Michigan Natural Features Inventory, Report Number 2007-21, Lansing: Michigan State University Board of Trustees, 2007.

Lynch, Patrick, J., and Proctor, Noble, S. *Manual of Ornithology, Avian Structure and Function*. New Haven: Yale University Press, 1993.

Perrins, C.M., ed., *Oxford Ornithology Series*. New York: Oxford University Press, 2002.

Podulka, S., Rohrbaugh, Jr., R.W., Bonny, R., eds. *Handbook of Bird Biology, Second Edition*, Ithaca: Cornell Lab of Ornithology; Princeton: Princeton University Press, 2004.

The Birds of North America Online (A. Poole, Ed.). Ithaca: Cornell Laboratory of Ornithology; Retrieved from The Birds of North American Online database: http://bna.birds.cornell.edu/BNA/; AUG 2005.

Saur, J.R., Hines, J.E., and Fallow, J. *The North American Breeding Bird Survey, Results and Analysis 1966–2004*. Laurel: USGS Patuxent Wildlife Research Center, 2005.

About the Author

Award-winning author and science educator Adele Porter combines her passion for science and dedication to children in her new books. In fact, the students that Adele has worked with during 20 years as an educator inspired *Wild About Michigan Birds*. Adele has also written educational materials for the Minnesota Department of Natural Resources, the U.S. Forest Service and various publications. She is a member of the National Science Teachers' Association, the American Ornithologists' Union, and the Society of Children's Book Writers and Illustrators.

For Adele, one of the best parts of being an author is meeting the readers of her books at author programs and book signings and hearing their enthusiastic outdoor adventure stories. She looks forward to hearing of your new wildlife adventures!

A native of Minnesota, Adele enjoys the time she and her three children spend together more than anything else. She can be contacted via her author website, www.adeleporter.com.

Go to www.birdsforkids.com to download and print a free bookmark that features a life-size Black-capped Chickadee and tells how to use your book to identify a bird!